STARLIGHT

STARLIGHT

VICTOR BOOKS ®
A DIVISION OF SCRIPTURE PRESS PUBLICATIONS INC.
USA CANADA ENGLAND

Scripture quotations marked (NIV) are taken from the Holy Bible, New International Version 1973, 1978, 1984, International Bible Society. Used by permission of Zondervan Bible Publishers. Other quotations are from the King James Version (KJV); The Living Bible, 1971, Tyndale House Publishers, Wheaton, IL 60189. Used by permission; and from J.B. Phillips: The New Testament in Modern English, Revised Edition, J.B. Phillips, 1958, 1960, 1972, permission of Macmillan Publishing Co. and Collins Publishers.

Recommended Dewey Decimal Classification: 222.9
Suggested Subject Heading: BIBLE, O.T.—ESTHER

Library of Congress Catalog Card Number: 87-62497
ISBN: 0-89693-465-9

VICTOR BOOKS
A division of SP Publications, Inc.
        Wheaton, Illinois 60l87

·CONTENTS·

CONTENTS

• INTRODUCTION •

How does God reach out of our lives and into the lives of others? Esther—the woman in an unbelieving environment, shows us how. The story of Esther is a story of kings and queens and commonplace ordinary people, who teach among other things, that kings' palaces are not necessarily the only place where royalty can be found. There's a majesty of spirit—lent to mortal man in touch with an immortal God—that makes a king or queen out of the most humble of His subjects. And there's a kingdom not of this earth, that other kingdoms however magnificent they may be, merely shadow. Subjects of this spiritual kingdom enamored of their King, dress splendidly in character's cloth; shiny fabric reflecting redemption, making them appear like stars. And such they are. So God hangs them up in dark forboding skies to point the way to home and heaven, where stars are born. This is the story of Esther whose name means "star," one of the brightest and best of them!

• BEFORE YOU BEGIN •

People who gather together for Bible study are likely to be at different places in their spiritual lives, and their study materials should be flexible enough to meet their different needs. This book is designed to be used as a Bible study guide for such groups in homes or churches. It can also be used by individuals who are studying on their own. The lessons are written in five distinct sections, so that they can be used in a variety of situations. Groups and individuals alike can choose to use the elements they find most useful in the order they find most beneficial.

These studies will help you learn some new truths from the Bible as well as how to dig out those truths. You will learn not only *what* the Bible says, but how to use Scripture to deepen your relationship with Jesus Christ by obeying it and applying it in daily living. These studies will also provide an opportunity for potential leaders to learn how to lead a discussion in a nonthreatening setting.

What You'll Need

For each study you will need a Bible and this Bible study guide. You might also want to have a notebook in which to record your thoughts and discoveries from your personal study and group meetings. A notebook could also be used to record prayer requests from the group.

The Sections

Food for Thought. This is a devotional narrative that introduces the topic, person, or passage featured in the lesson. There are several ways it can be used. Each person could read it before coming to the group meeting, and someone could briefly summarize it at the be ginning. It could be read silently by each person at the beginning of the session, or it could be read aloud, by one or several group members. (Suggested time: 10 minutes)

Talking It Over. This section contains discussion questions to help you review what you learned in Food for Thought. There are also questions to help you apply the narrative's truths to daily life. The person who leads the discussion of these questions need not be a trained or experienced teacher. All that is needed is someone to keep things moving and facilitate group interaction. (Suggested time: 30 minutes)

Praying It Through. This is a list of suggestions for prayer based on the lesson. You may want to use all the suggestions or eliminate some in order to leave more time for personal sharing and prayer requests. (Suggested time: 20 minutes)

Digging Deeper. The questions in this section are also related to the passage, topic, or character from the lesson. But they will not always be limited to the exact passage or character from Food for Thought. Passages and characters from both the Old and New Testaments will appear in this section, in order to show how God has worked through *all* of history in people's lives. These questions will require a little more thinking and some digging into Scripture, as well as some use of Bible study tools. Participants will be stretched as they become experienced in the "how-tos" of Bible study. (Suggested time: 45 minutes)

Tool Chest. The Tool Chest contains a description of a specific type of Bible study help and includes an explanation of how it is used. An example of the tool is given, and an example of it or excerpt from it is usually included in the Digging Deeper study.

The Bible study helps in the Tool Chest can be purchased by anyone who desires to build a basic library of Bible study reference books and other tools. They would also be good additions to a church library. Some are reasonably inexpensive, but others are quite expensive. A few may be available in your local library or in a seminary or college library. A group might decide to purchase one tool during each series and build a corporate tool chest for all the members of the group to use. You can never be too young a Christian to begin to master Bible study helps, nor can you be too old to learn new methods of rightly dividing the Word of truth.

Options for Group Use

Different groups, made up of people at diverse stages of spiritual growth, will want to use the elements in this book in different ways. Here are a few suggestions to get you started, but be creative and sensitive to your group's needs.

☐ Spend 5-15 minutes at the beginning of the group time introducing yourselves and having group members answer an icebreaker question. (Sample icebreaker questions are included under Tips for Leaders.)

☐ Extend the prayer time to include sharing of prayer requests, praise items, or things group members have learned recently in their times of personal Bible study.

☐ The leader could choose questions for discussion from the Digging Deeper section based on whether participants have prepared ahead of time or not.

☐ The entire group could break into smaller groups to allow different groups to use different sections. (The smaller groups could move to other rooms in the home or church where you are meeting.)

Tips for Leaders
Preparation

1. Pray for the Holy Spirit's guidance as you study, that you will be equipped to teach the lesson and make it appealing and applicable.

2. Read through the entire lesson and any Bible passages or verses that are mentioned. Answer all the questions.

3. Become familiar enough with the lesson that, if time in the

group is running out, you know which questions could most easily be left out.

4. Gather all the items you will need for the study: name tags, extra pens, extra Bibles.

The Meeting
1. Start and end on time.
2. Have everyone wear a name tag until group members know one another's names.
3. Have each person introduce himself or herself, or ask regular attenders to introduce guests.
4. For each meeting, pick an icebreaker question or another activity to help group members get to know one another better.
5. Use any good ideas to make everyone feel comfortable.

The Discussion
1. Ask the questions, but try to let the group answer. Don't be afraid of silence. Reword the question if it is unclear to the group or answer it yourself to clarify.
2. Encourage everyone to participate. If someone is shy ask that person to answer an opinion question or another nonthreatening question. If someone tends to monopolize the discussion, thank that person for his or her contribution and ask if someone else has anything he or she would like to add. (Or ask that person to make the coffee!)
3. If someone gives an incorrect answer, don't bluntly or tactlessly tell him or her so. If it is partly right, reinforce that. Ask if anyone else has any thoughts on the subject. (Disagree agreeably!)
4. Avoid tangents. If someone is getting off the subject, ask that person his or her point relates to the lesson.
5. Don't feel threatened if someone asks a question you can't answer. Tell the person you don't know but will find out before the next meeting—then be sure to find out! Or ask if someone would like to research and present the answer at the group's next meeting.

Icebreaker Questions
The purpose of these icebreaker questions is to help the peoplein your group get to know one another over the course of the study. The questions you use when your group members don't know one another very well should be very general and nonthreatening. As time goes on, your questions can become more focused and specific. Always give group members the option of passing if they think a

question is too personal.

What do you like to do for fun?
What is your favorite season? dessert? book?
What would be your ideal vacation?
What exciting thing happened to you this week?
What was the most memorable thing you did with your family when you were a child?
What one word best describes the way you feel today?
Tell three things you are thankful for.
Imagine that your house is on fire. What three things would you try to take with you on your way out?
If you were granted one wish, what would it be?
What experience of your past would you most enjoy reliving?
What quality do you most appreciate in a friend?
What is your pet peeve?
What is something you are learning to do or trying to get better at?
What is your greatest hope?
What is your greatest fear?
What one thing would you like to change about yourself?
What has been the greatest accomplishment of your life?
What has been the greatest disappointment of your life?

Need More Help?
Here is a list of books that contain helpful information on leading discussions and working in groups:

How to Lead Small Group Bible Studies (NavPress, 1982).
Creative Bible Learning for Adults, Monroe Marlowe and Bobbie Reed (Regal, 1977).
Getting Together, Em Griffin (InterVarsity Press, 1982).
Good Things Come in Small Groups (InterVarsity Press, 1985).

One Last Thought
This book is a tool you can use whether you have one or one hundred people who want to study the Bible and whether you have one or no teachers. Don't wait for a brilliant Bible study leader to appear—most such teachers acquired their skills by starting with a book like this and learning as they went along. Torrey said, "The best way to begin, is to begin." Happy beginnings!

11

1
God In The Shadows

•FOOD FOR THOUGHT•

In Esther's time the Jews remained in the various provinces of the Medo-Persian Empire rather than exercising their option to return to Jerusalem under Zerubbabel. God's people had prospered, being given a measure of freedom under King Xerxes. He had allowed them to practice many of their customs and laws in an empire that had become a moderately safe place to live. Many of God's people decided to stay and take their chances rather than uproot their families, leave their friends, and trek back to a ruined city and an uncertain future. Perhaps it is unfair to suggest that only the most pious of Israel's children returned to the Holy City, but if that were the case, it would appear that God had not left Himself without witness in the land of the Medes and Persians!

In the Book of Esther, Mordecai and Esther shine like stars in a dark sky. The author paints a wonderful portrait against a fabulous oriental landscape. The book is distinctly Persian; the names Mordecai and Esther are respectively the Persian names for "Marduk" (the War god of Babylon) and the "planet star Venus." I'm sure we will all be able to identify with the people we meet in these pages, particularly Esther, a woman who faced fascinatingly similar situations to those you and I face today.

At the time these events took place, Persia ruled the world and Rome was only a second rate Italian commonwealth. King Xerxes fought many a bloody conflict to tighten his grip on his kingdom. In his time, Egypt revolted only to be subdued, while the Greeks kept the king busy, frustrating his attempts to subdue them at the famous battles of Thermogylae, Artemus, and Salames.

To be a Jew in such a day and age meant dealing not only with the secular Jewish brother who had lost his vision and calling, but with wild Persian religions as well. There was also the influence of

Confucius and Buddha, who both died around this period.

So what do we know about Xerxes, or Ahasuerus (his Hebrew name) and his rule over such diverse peoples? We know his name spelled terror in the hearts of the people he ruled in 127 provinces from India to Ethiopia. We also know he was driven by his greed for money, sex, and power. The picture we are given is an ugly one. He treated his subdued peoples like cattle, raping their land and forcing them to pay tribute and taxes to fund his wild military campaigns. He was a crude man and a most materialistic minded king.

When Haman, the Jew-hater, persuaded Xerxes to exterminate all the Jews, he achieved Xerxes' complicity with the offer of 10,000 talents (Es. 3:9). Since the annual income of the whole Persian empire was only 15,000 talents, two-thirds of that amount must have tempted the money minded monarch into compliance with such a diabolical plot. After agreeing to the plan, the two conspirators drank to it, a callous example of vicious cold-blooded men out for all they could get (Es. 3:15). Apparently, money meant a great deal to Xerxes—more than his marriage, more than his princes and friends, in fact, more than anything!

Money, sex, and power . . . these words have a modern ring to them. Let's think about "power" for a moment. Sometimes money can buy power, but Xerxes didn't have to rely solely on the ability to buy the world. He was certainly not adverse to using force. To friends and foes alike he was a dangerous man. He would fly into fits of diabolical rage for the most childish of reasons. For example, on the way to Greece, Xerxes met an influential man of Lydia named Pythias. Not only had Pythias given Xerxes an incredibly generous contribution for his Greek military campaign, but all but one of his sons had served the king. When the old man begged Xerxes to allow his one remaining son to stay home and support him in his old age, Xerxes flew into an uncontrollable rage, ordering the son in question to be cut into pieces for his army to march between!

Perhaps we get the best glimpse of Xerxes' character at a palace party where Xerxes wanted to show off his wealth. The event was apparently orchestrated in order to impress the Satraps of the 127 provinces, thus ensuring support for his Greek campaign.

The beautiful and ornate Persian palace at Susa lent itself well to Xerxes' garden party, the likes and lengths of which few had experienced before. The party lasted 180 days, and the drinking began to have its effect! Xerxes decided to satisfy his vanity and pride by parading his beautiful wife, Vashti, before his guests.

At the same time, Vashti, not to be outdone by the king, had put

13

on her own "bash" for the ladies of the provinces. In the middle of the festivities the king's eunuchs arrived and summoned the queen to the king's garden. Though his harem was amply furnished with concubines, Xerxes apparently had the idea of commanding Vashti to expose herself to his guests so his subjects could envy him.

Vashti, however, was Xerxes' match. The queen, whether from pride or prudence, refused to parade herself before the drunken men. Thus she dishonored her king and bravely sent a message to the world that her marriage was a mess. Brave, foolish, or perhaps a little bit drunk, Vashti found herself the victim of Memucan and the king's advisors, and was summarily divorced (Es. 1:19).

What parallels can we draw? Perhaps we can talk about submission. To submit or not to submit; *that* is the question. Must a wife submit to any old thing? Scripture leads us to conclude that a husband should not be absolute or autocratic. His government or headship must be within limits fixed by the Lord Himself, for no husband has the right to command a wife to do that which is wrong.

The Bible says that when the eunuchs returned bearing Vashti's succinct negative, the king "frothed at the mouth and became like a wild boar" (Es. 1:12). I talked to a young wife once who refused to go with her husband to a wife-swapping party. Faced with her refusal, her husband lost control. Like Vashti, this young woman found herself under the threat of divorce. Vashti, however, faced more than a threat. She found herself divorced on the spot and replaced within a very short time. It's not easy to be married to a Xerxes even when you are not a believer like Vashti and play by the same rules. It's a great deal harder to know what to do when your name is Esther and you belong to God! But that part of the story must wait!

A word about Memucan, the king's counselor. Most of us have experienced his kind of advice. When our marriages are in trouble, someone is usually on hand to offer his view on the subject. If Vashti went unpunished, Memucan feared that she would prove to be a very bad example for all the other wives of the realm. Taking his cue from the "norms" of his own society, Memucan callously advised the king to get rid of his wife. There are many "Memucans" who have served to add to the misery and mess of our present day marriage problems. We must be careful where we go for counsel when our relationships get into trouble. When the king's wrath eventually subsided, he was sorry for his hasty action, but it was too late. If we would only "cool it" in similar circumstances and seek God's council and help, then many a marriage might be saved.

The gripping story of Esther is very applicable for us today, yet one outstanding feature of this book is the complete absence of a single reference to God Himself. Some scholars think that the author wrote in this way to heighten the fact that it is God who controls all seemingly insignificant happenings of life. God's sovereign rule must be assumed at every point in the story. In fact, it has been said that in no other book of the Bible is He "seen" more clearly. For God is a "person" infinitely interested in us "personally." This unique Scripture gives us great encouragement when we face a dark night and have to use our "eyes of faith" to see Him in the shadows.

God's providence is His presence and His power to turn any circumstances to His own account. We are about to watch Him use this particular colorful episode to introduce Esther to the king and establish her influence for good and for God! He is also intent on blessing us as He works out His ultimate plan and purpose for mankind. And what is that plan and purpose? To set the stage of history for the entrance of Jesus Christ, the Saviour of the world.

Jesus Himself told us that "salvation is from the Jews" (John 4:22), and God reveals His unseen activity in Esther's day through her unique circumstances preserving the nation that would give the Saviour to the world. Mordecai reminded Esther as she faced the challenge of her life, "you have come to royal position for such a time as this" (Es. 4:14).

Have you ever looked at your particular situation and realized that God wants to use you on the stage of history in a way similar to the way He used Esther? People are dying in the darkness, and He wants to hang us up like stars at night to bring attention to the Light of the world—Jesus! What a sense of worth it brings us, to realize that like Esther we are center stage in God's thinking . . . for just "such a time as this!"

God wants us to be happy - thats part of His plan for us.

•TALKING IT OVER•

---

1. REVIEW AND DISCUSS.   *15 minutes*

☐ What would have been hard about living in Persia in Esther's time? Start your sentence with "I would not have liked . . ."

☐ By living in the U.S.A. today, what advantages do you have over Esther?

☐ What struck you most about each of the following people?
Xerxes
Vashti
Memucan

---

2. DISCUSS TOGETHER AND SHARE.   *15 minutes*

☐ Compare King Xerxes' party with parties today. Discuss any similarities.

☑ Do you think Vashti was right or wrong to refuse the King's request?

☐ Which of the following words best describes Vashti?

| proud | brave | right |
| stupid | beautiful | wrong |

☑ Should Christian women always submit to their Christian husbands?

☑ Who should single women submit to? God

☐ Share an experience where, in retrospect you can see God was standing in the shadows.

•PRAYING IT THROUGH•

1. (On your own) Praise God's Person, Providence, and Plan.
   Praise God for all the things from this lesson that have helped you.

   2 minutes

2. (On your own) Pray for:
   ☐ Men you know like Xerxes.
   ☐ Women you know like Vashti.
   ☐ Counselors you know like Memucan.

   3 minutes

3. (In twos) Share a "dark" situation you may be in. Pray for each other that you will be God's star.

   15 minutes

•DIGGING DEEPER•

Esther should be read and studied as a story. This does not mean that the book of Esther is fictitious. Neither does it lack historical and theological accuracy. It does mean that Esther contains the elements which make up most stories. Examining these elements will help us better understand the author's intended purpose for writing Esther. As you read Esther from beginning to end in one sitting, observe the following story elements.

Setting
1. In what time period and location is the story of Esther set?

   483 B.C. in Persia

   Does the setting give any clues as to what kind of action might occur?

   Specifically, where does the action take place?

   the palace

   Does the setting reveal the social status of the characters?

   very wealthy

   Is anything else about the characters indicated by the setting?

   Do you recognize any symbolic significance behind the setting?

Narration
2. Is this story told in first person or by a narrator?

   narrator

   Who is the narrator of the story?

   Mordecai

How does the narrator view his characters? Is it ever possible to determine how he feels about them by the words he selects to describe the characters and the events? What is his attitude toward the main characters, the Jews and the Persians?

Plot

3. Plot refers to the events an author includes in a story and their arrangement. In what chapters does the main action occur? What events have been included in Esther?

Which events have been omitted and why?

What is the order of events?

How have these events been ordered? (i.e. chronologically, causally) Are any of the events told out of sequence? Do any occur unexpectedly?

Is suspense used to develop the story? If so, where and what means are employed to build suspense?

What do you believe to be the goal of the story?

Climax

4. The climax of a story is when the major character either achieves or fails at attaining his goal. Who is the central figure in the story?

Identify his/her goal.

What obstacle(s) interfere(s) with the achievement of that goal?

How is this resolved?

What is the climax of the book of Esther?

Twist

5. Were there any unusual surprises you noted in the action when reading Esther?

How many twists did you observe? How did each twist relate to the events of the story preceding it?

Characters

6. Identify the four primary characters in the book. What do they do? Are they good or evil? How do they change over time?

Xerxes
Vashti
Esther
Mordecai

Did your attitude change toward any of them? If so, at what point?

List the other characters and describe how each relates to the plot.

Symbols

7. A symbol can be an object, event, or action which points to something besides itself. Did you find any symbols in Esther?

What might the feasts represent?

To what might the fasts refer?

Theme
8. What are the prevalent themes in this story? Look for repeating words, phrases, and ideas to help answer this question.

Purpose
9. From your first impressions and initial study, what do you think might be the purpose behind the book of Esther? In other words, why was it written?

10. Is God telling a story through you? Identify the story elements in your own life.

Setting

Narrator

Plot

Climax

Twists

Characters

Symbols

Themes

What is God's purpose for your story?

For Further Study
1. Reread Esther and isolate the individual scenes, their beginning, end, and how they relate to one another.

•TOOL CHEST•
(A Suggested Optional Resource)

STUDY BIBLES

The first major addition to your personal library should be a study Bible. Browse through your church library or Christian bookstore and decide what translation is most suitable for you. Although a paraphrase is often the most readable choice, a paraphrase is not the most accurate. When looking for a study Bible take into consideration readability and understandability, objective study notes, cross references, concordance size, illustrations, maps, and other helps. Compare Bibles to determine the right one for you. I suggest you borrow a friend's Bible for a week and pray about your selection. This decision will probably be the most important in setting up your library. The following is a representative list of the study Bibles available today:

The New International Study Bible (Zondervan Bible Publishers)
The Open Bible (Thomas Nelson Publishers)
The Thompson Chain-Reference Bible (Zondervan Bible Publishers)

2

A Star Is Born

•FOOD FOR THOUGHT•

On March 23, 1987, Time magazine featured the story of "Supernova," the brightest exploding star in 383 years! "Suddenly," said the caption under the picture of the incredible ball of light, "it flared into view shining with the brilliance of a 100 million stars." The article spoke of different kinds of stars, like the white dwarf for instance, and tried to explain to simple minded men and women, the complexity of their make up, and what it took to create those particular phenomena.

Esther was surely one of God's supernovas! There is no doubt about it that God used her to create just as much attention in her world, that the 1987 supernova created in ours!

As I tried to grasp what the article was all about, I noticed that one particular theme kept reoccurring--a supernova only occurs when a star dies! A star dies when it uses up all its fuel and collapses "in" on itself creating so much pressure that incredible forces are released that eventually cause it's demise. I felt quite sorry for the dying star, yet I realized that the photographs made me want to take up stargazing!

Do you want to be a spiritual supernova? If your answer is yes, you need to realize that constant, unbearable breaking forces will enter your life, creating changes and preventing you from becoming a white dwarf! O for the spiritual passion and desire that pressures us to dare to say to the Lord, "Bring such forces into our souls, whether internally or through the forces of circumstance, so that You make us stars to be reckoned with!"

There is no question about it; many people in the Persian empire ended up stargazing at Queen Esther. The time was around 483 B.C., and Vashti, Queen of Persia, had been deposed. Refusing the king's command that she publicly expose herself in a lewd manner,

Vashti's behavior was perceived as a threat to all the men of the realm. Brutal repression of the women in the kingdom resulted, recommended by the king's counsel who was concerned that the domestic situation might get out of hand. Some historians believe that Vashti was as cruel and calculating as Xerxes himself, and that even he was intimidated by her. However, her bold refusal to "dance like a monkey" for the king at his party brought about her downfall, and in the providence of God set the stage of history for Esther's entrance!

Working behind the scenes of Persian life, God cared for His child, the adopted daughter of Mordecai. When the heat is on and we are in the middle of the drama, it's hard to realize God is doing anything at all on our behalf. It is usually only in retrospect that we see He was there all the time.

Esther, a servant of the true God in a land of dark idolatry, teaches us many lessons. For example, she appears to have been able to live with her past. Many Christians say, "I can't shine today because of yesterday's darkness." Their past seems to chain them, and they are unable to cope with their present problems because of it. Esther had plenty of reasons to be bitter about her past, but her theology enabled her to understand the "big picture," and this perspective helped her to cope effectively with the present.

Esther would certainly have had the advantage of having access to a rich religious heritage. It is very possible that she, along with many other Jews of the dispersion, were well aware of the prophet Daniel's writings and ministry. Though Daniel finished his book around the fall of Babylon, 60-70 years before Esther was born, it was close enough in time for his messages to have had an impact on the Jewish community in Persia. His miraculous preservation in the den of lions must certainly have been well known, serving to encourage the scattered people of God as well as Esther who was about to face her own breed of ferocious animals!

In Daniel 2, one of Nebuchadnezzar's dreams had to do with a large statue (representing four successive world empires) and a confederacy that would prove to be weak and vulnerable. In the dream, a stone cut without hands suddenly appeared striking the great statue at its feet and destroying it all together. Then the stone grew and grew until it filled the earth. Daniel interpreted the King's dream, saying that King Nebuchadnezzar represented the mighty head of the statue. We know now through history that the silver torso of the figure might well represent the Persians; the bronze thighs, Greece; and the iron legs, Rome. We can presume that we live in a time very close to the entrance of Jesus (the stone cut without hands), who will return to this earth to establish His kingdom.

Daniel's prophetic message must have helped the Israelites see that God is sovereign in the affairs of men, and that "the king's heart is in the hand of the Lord; He directs it like a watercourse wherever He pleases" (Prov. 21:1). When you are dealing with your past, it helps to realize that your past as well as your present and future are all part of the "big picture" that God is busy painting. He is working His purposes out and will eventually "reign for ever and ever" (Rev. 11:15). If we can remember that the kingdoms of this world will eventually become "the kingdom of our Lord and of His Christ" (v. 15), it will make it a little easier to deal with some of the hard things that have happened to us.

We can also remind ourselves that we could have been unfortunate enough to be born under a Nebuchadnezzar or Xerxes, or even a Nero, rather than living in a democratic, modern civilization. But this can be cold comfort to those who struggle with a disastrous past. However, if we get our theology straight and come to believe that we are all part of God's purposes which most surely *will* come to a predetermined end, it will make it a little easier to understand the big picture. We must believe that God *is* in control, even if we are tempted to believe that He has been disinterested in us as individuals.

"Why didn't He intervene?" a friend asked me in a bewildered fashion, recounting dreadful childhood abuse she had suffered. "It's as if He was standing there watching my suffering with His hands in His pockets!" If we are not to make God look like an impersonal deity, far removed from a loving concern for His creatures, we will need to be able to convince people that this concept of God is far from the truth. The story of Daniel and Esther helps us to believe that fact.

After we have our theology straight regarding God's overall plan for the world, we need to grasp the fact that God has a personal plan for *our* lives too. The Bible teaches us we are not pawns but people, and God cares individually and compassionately about each and everyone of us. If we can believe this we will stop looking at ourselves as victims and become victors over our circumstances instead.

But how do we get the right ideas about God? Where do we find the information that will rightly instruct us concerning His character? From the written Word of God. As we systematically work our way through the Bible, an understanding of God's purpose and character will become clear to us. We will not be able to escape the realization that Jesus was God in human flesh who came to complete the Father's eternal plan on the cross. That is the big part of the big picture! But Jesus also spent many moments healing lepers, talking one on one with needy individuals, and telling us He loved and cared about us. This was the personal part of His plan!

So once we have the sense of God's eminence—His size and His immediate presence—we will have a far better perspective through which to look at our memories and come to terms with them.

We need to let God wipe the tears from the eyes of our memories! As a child of the dispersion, Esther must have done a lot of crying. Though she was probably born in Persia, her parents had apparently died while she was young. To be an orphan, refugee, and a female, was not a very good idea in the year 408 B.C.! But I believe Esther allowed God to wipe the tears from the eyes of her memories. I don't believe the good attitudes of this beautiful girl that we glean from Esther 2 could have flourished in bitter soil. In retrospect, Esther must have been able to see God clearly in the shadows of her life. Surely it was He that provided her with a loving uncle to parent and protect her.

Are you obsessed by memories from a bitter childhood? Have you lost family and home; been displaced; mistreated? Have you ever asked God to wipe the tears from the eyes of your memories? You may ask how healing happens. One of the answers lies in prayer. The Bible tells us just Who to turn to with our hurts. It is prayer that takes us to the right place!

Of course, dealing with our past helps us to cope with our present. By looking back and accepting the things that happened to us as simply part of life lived in a fallen world that is waiting for its redemption, we can more easily accept the things that are happening to us in our present. Accepting things we cannot change about our past helps us to accept things we cannot change about our present situation too.

For example, Esther couldn't bring her parents back from death so she could have a "normal" family life. She couldn't escape Xerxes harem either! She was powerless to do anything about her present dilemma, just as she had been powerless to do anything about the problems of her past. Scripture tells us she had been "taken by force" into the king's harem just as her family had been taken by force into Babylonia.

The king was away at the time the maidens were sought out and assembled for his pleasure. He was trying to teach the Greeks a lesson for soundly defeating his father at the battle of Marathon.

Meanwhile, his henchmen had provided a harem full of the best beauties of Persia's far flung empire. Esther had not been able to choose her childhood guardian, and she was certainly not invited to willingly say "I do" to her nuptial partner either! This was a situation she could do absolutely nothing about save accept!

When you find yourself in a situation you cannot change, ask God to help you to accept it. I am *not* saying don't try to change a bad scene. What I am saying is when you find yourself in a bind that is impossible to do anything about, try and come to terms with it for "in acceptance lieth peace."

As a young wife of a youth worker who traveled extensively, I realized that I couldn't control my circumstances. Coming to terms with that meant accepting it in prayer and asking God to help me to maximize the situation. This resulted in me being able to stop wasting precious energy that I needed to survive the stress by playing "I wish it could be different" games. I began turning resources into more creative pursuits.

Esther soon became the most popular girl in the harem! She charmed Hegai, the eunuch in charge of the harem, the women themselves, and, incredibly, she charmed Xerxes too! "Now the king was attracted to Esther more than to any of the other women, and she won his favor and approval more than any of the other virgins. So he set a royal crown on her head and made her queen instead of Vashti" (Es. 2:17).

Esther's environment was influenced by more than mere beauty of form or strength of character. I believe her environment was impacted by her life of disciplined obedience learned from her youth, married to a fragrant faith in God whom she believed would be faithful to her no matter what. God's power can be let loose through such a trusting believer!

Having dealt with her past and coped with her present dilemma, all that remained for Esther was to trust God for her future. Can you imagine taking a whole year to prepare for a night in bed with Xerxes? Seeing he had recently returned home from a thorough beating at the battle of Salosus, he could hardly have been in a very good mood! Also, Esther was a virgin, and the king no doubt very experienced in sexual matters. All of this knowledge wouldn't have helped her wedding night nerves.

Is God relevant when we find ourselves in awful situations like this? Yes, the Bible says that God was relevant in Esther's life. We read that the king loved her more than all the other women and made her his queen. It is interesting to note that the feast Xerxes proclaimed as part of the celebrations for his new bride was very different from Vashti's feast. Esther's feast was an occasion to set prisoners free, forgive debtors, and provide for the needy. As soon as God hung His star in place it began to shine brightly! Esther's influence had begun to make its mark!

What dreaded event do you fear in the future? Will you believe in the God of Esther who will meet you around the corner of tomorrow and give you the power to live a day at a time for His glory? I agree that being a supernova will require supernatural strength, but that is exactly what our God has promised to supply!

God's "lights" have come to terms with their past, maximized their present and faced their future with a faith that chases fear away! Don't be a white dwarf in a black hole! Be a supernova for God!

•TALKING IT OVER•

---

1. DISCUSS TOGETHER.   *5 minutes*
   ☐ Do you feel like a supernova, a white dwarf, or
   a black hole?
   ☐ How do internal pressures and outside forces
   produce bright lights in the Christian life?

---

2. SHARE.   *8 minutes*
   ☐ Which part of today's story challenged you
   most and why?
   Dealing with the past?
   Coping with the present?
   Facing the future?

---

3. READ AND DISCUSS IN TWOS.   *10 minutes*
   Study Daniel's dream in Daniel 2.
   ☐ Identify the names of the different empires.
   ☐ What did the stone cut without hands do? What
   do you think it might represent?
   ☐ In which period do you think Esther lived?
   What does that "say" to you?

---

4. REFLECT.   *7 minutes*
   How does Scripture and prayer help us to be supernovas? Read a verse from chapter 2 out loud
   and pray about it.

•PRAYING IT THROUGH•

*Suggested
Times*

1. (As a group) Praise God for being Creator of the physical universe (Ps. 19:1).
   ☐ Praise God for supernova Christians who have lit up your dark sky.
   ☐ Praise God for the pressures that help us die to ourselves in order that we may live for Him.

5 minutes

2. (As a group) Pray for:

orphans	abused women
single parents	single girls
refugees	God's people under fire

   10 minutes

3. (On your own) Read Esther 2. Close your eyes and picture it all. Talk to God about what you "see." How do some of the lessons we have learned apply to you?

5 minutes

•DIGGING DEEPER•

Xerxes

1. Pick out phrases from 1:1-8 which portray the vast extent of Xerxes rule.

How many banquets did King Xerxes throw?

How much time has passed in the first eight verses of the book?

What motivation might have been behind such extravagant affairs?

Positive:

Negative:

Are you ever so generous? Do you show off your vanity?

What hint does the text give us about the atmosphere of the banquets? (vv. 8, 10)

Why did the author choose to begin his story with these events?

2. Who were the guests at Vashti's banquet?

What do you learn about Queen Vashti in verses 9-12?

Imagine yourself in Vashti's position. What might have provoked you to refuse the King?

3. Skim the rest of chapter one and read 2:1. What do you learn about the king's nature?

How many men did it take to attend the King? To advise him?

What is unusual about his request in 1:15?

4. Outline Memucan's reply:

What reason does he give for Vashti's severe sentence?

5. What impressions do you get from 2:1-14 that the king is hard to please?

In what ways are you more like Xerxes than you would like to admit? Give an example.

6. Why is it surprising that 3:1 immediately follows the episode in 2:19-23? What would you have expected to read?

Now read 6:1-3. What strikes you as odd?

What can you deduce about Xerxes from these events?

7. More of the king's character is revealed in 6:3-11. Add these attributes to the description you began in exercise 3.

8. Number the banquets the king attends for Esther. What does this imply about him?

How would you categorize his response to Esther's petition in 7:5, 7?

What could account for his surprise?

Why does he enter the garden?

What lesson can you learn from Xerxes' lack of attention to detail? Are you ever guilty of the same?

9. List the ways Xerxes remedied the situation:

7:9-10

8:1, 15

8:2

8:11

8:13

Is there a situation in your life in which you have erred? How should you remedy it?

10. What is King Xerxes remembered for in the closing verses of Esther?

What one word would you use to sum up Xerxes?

For what will you be remembered? For what would you like to be remembered?

What changes need to happen in your life for this to be true?

For Further Study
1. Read an article on Xerxes (Ahasuerus) in a Bible dictionary and add to your character study of Xerxes any new discoveries you find.

•TOOL CHEST•
(A Suggested Optional Resource)

BIBLE DICTIONARIES
Have you ever struggled with the meaning of an unusual word, name, or place in Scripture? Perhaps you have often wondered how to pronounce a name or city. Maybe you prefer to think visually, and you have tried to picture the topography of Bible lands, or what the Temple must have looked like. A Bible dictionary can assist you in these discoveries and many more. It will become a close companion during your personal study times and in message preparation. These tools come in paperback or hard cover and range from $5.00 to $25.00. A very good evangelical text is *The New Bible Dictionary* (Tyndale). Thorough in its background information but less conservative in its theology is *Harper's Bible Dictionary* (Harper and Row).

3

The Darkening Sky

•FOOD FOR THOUGHT•

God writes the course of world events across the pages of history including a dramatic chapter of Esther's life where she finds herself married to a man she couldn't have imagined herself marrying! Most of us really marry strangers, regardless of how long we have known our partners before the wedding. It's marriage that reveals us to each other. In the northern part of England where I come from, there is a saying, "You never know what you've got, till you've got them home and the door shut!" Well if it is to be so in the normal course of events in modern day England, it was certainly so in Esther's case! Unlike us, she had no choice in the matter of mate and found herself married to a total stranger, a man she actually met on her "wedding night"! What a challenge!

Having started her married life in a rather unorthodox way, the beautiful Hadassah began to discover the real man behind the throne of Persia. It must have been somewhat of an unpleasant discovery. Not only did she find herself belonging to a complete stranger, she discovered him to be a most difficult man! It has been said that "the man exalted to the pedestal of a god is made dizzy by his own altitude!" King Xerxes had the most childish concept of his own supreme sense of importance. Esther was not the first, and neither would she be the last, to take stock of her situation and wonder how on earth she was going to cope!

Perhaps this rings a responsive note in your heart. Maybe you find yourself married to a stranger—a childish, proud, or unpredictable man. Perhaps you married him before you found Christ. Esther's biggest dilemma, like yours, was the fact that the man she had married was not saved. He was totally lost. Lost men like Xerxes are very little men in God's eyes though often very large in their own estimation of themselves. Are you married to an unbeliever? In

38

Christ, childish people can grow into maturity and be lent coping powers in many a relationship that would be doomed unless the believing wife made the difference. But it's hard to believe you can make a difference in the face of proud agnosticism.

God's creation is exquisite. Everything He makes is *very* good. The sun, moon, and stars He hung in the sky on the day of creation are no exception! His stars are stunningly beautiful. One aspect of the stars in the heavens that catches our breath is their incredible diversity. There is great beauty in diversity. Isn't this why every giraffe sports different patterns, every snowflake falls to the ground in a different shape, and even each nose on each human face has its own distinct features!

Esther found herself lined up in that ancient beauty pageant with a variety of beauties. Each girl taken forcibly into the king's harem to be readied for his bed bore beauty lightly and easily. Some according to their race would be dark and haughty, others light skinned and skittish. Esther, the flower of Jewish grace, would be as fair in form and face as all the rest. But there was more to Esther than form and face.

Esther was not only stunningly beautiful but spiritually beautiful too. I believe it was this quality of spiritual beauty that set her apart from all the other lovelies of the realm. God's spirit shone through the shell and captivated everyone.

A beauty of spirit sets the believer apart. Perhaps it is the peace that God gives that soothes the worried brow (and in so doing, keeps the wrinkles at bay!). Or maybe it is the startling purity that lights the eyes from within, giving them the color of Christlike character. All I know is that those who believe in Jesus are "beautiful" whatever their form or face. But when you have beauty in body as well as beauty in Spirit, you undoubtedly have the most winning combination! Esther was so endowed that when her turn came to go to the king, she took only what Hegai suggested (Es. 2:15). This means she went without the "trappings" of beauty that were the custom of the day. She made the very best of her particular gifts and left the rest to the Lord.

There are one or two reasons why she may have done this. Perhaps she didn't want the job, and she was therefore not going to be competitive! Then again, perhaps she knew that a competitive pushy spirit is not very feminine or beautiful. This does not for a moment mean Esther was not a strong person willing to excel at her job, but the spiritual beauty of a quiet submissive spirit is highly praised by men and must have contrasted dramatically with the spirit of Queen Vashti.

The Greek historian Herodotus tells us Queen Vashti matched the king in games of gross cruelty. Once in a fit of rage over her husband's affair with his brother's wife and daughter, she ordered her sister-in-law's nose and ears severed off her face and her tongue torn out! Maybe even a king as cruel as Xerxes was ready for a change after that!

When you are married to an unbeliever and are trying to win him to Christ, try a good dose of 1 Peter 3:1. Notice how the beauty of a meek and quiet spirit captivates a man's heart and wins his favor. Though Haggai and Xerxes could not have fully understood the difference between Esther and the surrounding beautiful women, God used his little star to shine right out into the darkness of their hearts and ensure she became Queen of Persia.

Janet, the girl who led me to Jesus was pretty! But ask me why and I couldn't really tell you. She had two eyes, a nose, a mouth, and black curly hair arranged together in a very pleasant face. But the face was not a mask; there was a vivaciousness, a spark, an added dimension—in fact, the light of God! It attracted me, and I found I couldn't look away. That star pointed me to Christ.

> God in the shadows hangs stars in the skies.
> He cleans up our souls, He lights up our eyes.
> So people who grope through the dusk of despair
> Begin to have hope and ask if He's there!
> He uses His starlets to show forth His glory,
> To drive away doubt, to shout out His story,
> To grapple with sin, and travel this earth,
> To shine out for Jesus with the joy of New Birth!

Having looked at God's beautiful star, Esther, let's look now at the darkening sky! Have you ever wondered why stars only come out at night? God wants them to shine especially brightly! Maybe it's because—

> You can't shine in a blue sky,
> But shine in the dark and He'll light up your eyes.
> God can't dry your tears if you never weep,
> Can't straighten you out if you're not in a heap!
> The blacker the background, the greater the chance
> To draw folks attention, the Lord to enhance.
> You can't shine in a blue sky,

When morning's broken, and sun is high.
But wait till the shadows of life lay you low,
Then Jesus will light you and set you aglow.

You can't shine in a blue sky! God allowed the shadows to length-
en and the day to flee away in order to have the perfect backdrop to
set off His jewel. "But," some of you might object, "It's so hard!
How can I be expected to shine when I'm hung up with an unbeliever? Divided loyalties are tearing me apart!"

Esther must have wrestled with this issue also. She surely struggled with divided loyalties as some of us do! Finding herself
(through no fault of her own) married to the king, she knew she
must try to please him and apparently succeeded! On the other
hand, there was another allegiance that claimed her heart. Every
good Jew knew that Jehovah, the King of the Universe, called His
children to love Him first and to obey His rules and laws. King
Xerxes certainly considered himself reason enough to be worshiped
heart and soul, so what did Esther do with her divided heart?

When you can't share the deepest and most significant part of
your life with your partner, problems build up in the relationship.
But even if you cannot share, you *can* care. We will see how Esther
coped with her divided life, love, and loyalty. When she could
submit, she did; when she could love, she would; when she had
opportunity to prove her allegiance to her monarch and obey his
earthly laws as long as they did not contravene the law of her God,
she was submissive and obedient! Mordecai her uncle behaved
likewise.

It happened that Mordecai had a position of influence in the
palace. Regardless of whether this position was given to him because
of Esther, Mordecai stumbled on a plot to kill the king (Es. 2:21-
22). He told Esther about it, and she warned Xerxes, giving her
uncle the credit. Unknown to anyone, God was busy writing the
script, bringing both Queen Esther and Mordecai into favor with
Xerxes and setting them in place for the next dramatic scene.

Beyond the bigger piece of the eternal puzzle lies an interesting
question: Why did Esther tell Xerxes about the plot on his life? I
can't help thinking that if I had been Esther, I wouldn't have both-
ered! It can't have been too much fun trying to love such a lecherous
man, and Mordecai would have had his own good reasons for releasing Esther from her obligations. But Esther and Mordecai didn't let
Bigthana and Teresh following through with their assassination
plans; Esther and Mordecai cared. In fact, if they hadn't cared so

much, I wonder what part they would have played in the deliverance of the Jews!

There are many loving, protective, and practical things we can do to show we care for the unbelievers in our lives; things that will build bridges over the chasms of our differences into their lives. These bridges may be essential to turn events in God's direction in the future. It was most certainly the case in Mordecai and Esther's experience.

So God hung his beautiful stars—Esther and Mordecai—high in the darkening sky. Shining brightly as only God's best can, they glittered with integrity.

The fact that Mordecai had instructed Esther not to reveal her identity does not show cowardice but rather prudence on their part (Es. 2:20). There is a time to stay silent, and there is a time to speak. God would direct such witness in His own good time, and He would make sure that they would have no doubt knowing when that witness should be made.

When God hangs us up among unbelievers, it's sometimes hard knowing when to speak and when to stay silent. Let Esther remind us to be obedient to the prompting of the Holy Spirit. Mordecai gives us a lovely picture of the Holy Spirit's work in this regard. Even as Mordecai prompted Esther when to keep silent and when to speak, the Holy Spirit will show us exactly the right moment to reveal our identity and stand up to be counted.

But now look at the gloomy horizon. Another light has appeared. A star—that shines with a different element endeavoring to outshine God's light. Haman has burst on the world stage like a gaudy shooting star, demanding attention, blinding the King, seeking to obliterate all the competition along the way (Es. 3:8-9).

The King, unable to discern good from evil, is captivated by the grand display of Haman's blazing trail and welcomes him warmly into the inner circle of his approval, exalting the man above all but himself. Haman, the supreme Jew-hater of all time, is about to make his presence felt!

The devil has his substitutes. He apes God and sometimes appears as an angel of light. The Jewish peoples scattered throughout the Persian empire sat down to supper oblivious of the fact that night had fallen, and that plans for the extermination were about to become a hideous reality. Esther, sleeping soundly in her bed in the queen's palace, was likewise unaware that the time was coming when she would "rise and shine" for her time had come!

•TALKING IT OVER•

---

1. SHARE.   *10 minutes*
   ☐ Esther found herself married to an unbeliever. If that has been your experience, share, if appropriate, one of the hard things about it.

---

2. READ AND DISCUSS TOGETHER.   *20 minutes*
   Read 1 Peter 3:1-7.
   ☐ What does this passage say to us?
   ☐ What parallels can we draw from Esther's story? Read the following passages about Daniel and Joseph.
   Genesis 41:37-40
   Daniel 1:18-20
   Daniel 2:46-49
   ☐ These men were yoked together with unbelievers in business and personal life. Discuss their lifestyles.
   ☐ How do the responses of those who are close to them encourage you?

• PRAYING IT THROUGH •

Suggested Times

---

1. (On your own) Praise God for the believers in your life.
   ☐ Praise God for the unbelievers in your life.

5 minutes

---

2. (As a group) Pray for unbelieving husbands to find the Lord.
   unbelieving children
   unbelieving friends
   unbelieving colleagues

10 minutes

---

3. (As a group) Pray about Haman's influence in your environment.
   ☐ Pray for people who are blinded by Satan's counterfeit stars.
   ☐ Pray quietly for yourself.

5 minutes

•DIGGING DEEPER•

Esther

1. How and why is Esther introduced to Xerxes court?

What event in chapter one served as the catalyst for her introduction?

How did Hegai show his favoritism for Esther?

What does the number of maids chosen to serve the new queen remind you of from lesson two? What do you think the author is emphasizing by symbolically using the number seven?

What does Hegai's favor toward Esther lead you to surmise about the future?

Read 2:5-18 and contrast your observations of Esther with those of Vashti from lesson two.

Similarities: *Dissimilarities:*

What have you learned so far about Esther's character?

2. How does Esther further display her obedience in this story?

2:10

2:20

2:22

4:15-16

In chapter 2, how might this story have ended, had Esther disobeyed Mordecai?

What was God teaching Esther during her early days in the Persian court?

Share an experience when you had to obey without having your whys answered. What did you learn?

3. Read 4:1-11. What threat does Mordecai bring to Esther's attention?

Is Esther's reply to her uncle's request one of disobedience?

Why does she hesitate?

What two-fold threat faces Esther?

What do you learn about Persian law from Esther's reply?

4. What does Mordecai believe will specifically happen to Esther if she refuses to comply?

What is Esther's predicament?

Whom will she obey and disobey (4:16) if she presents herself to the King?

From your study of Xerxes in lesson two, how is he likely to respond?

What does Mordecai conclude will happen to the Jewish nation if she refuses?

How can Mordecai be confident of this?

Why has there been no mention of God in this story?

5. From Esther's second reply to her uncle, what does she expect to be the outcome of her unsummoned appearance before the King?

Is a role reversal taking place in 4:15-17? Explain your answer.

What is unusual about *who* is going to fast? How could Esther include them?

Why did Esther call for a fast?

When is it appropriate for us to fast? Have you ever taken advantage of an appropriate opportunity to do so? What was the outcome?

6. Describe how Esther must have felt when the miracle of 5:1-3 occurred.

Why didn't Esther present her request immediately while the King was so pleased to see her?

What story element from lesson one do you recognize here?

Why does Esther continue to stall at her first banquet?

7. How many scenes occur between Esther's first and second banquets? What twists develop?

What do Esther's two banquets recall? What story element is involved?

8. What two questions does Xerxes ask, and what two answers does Esther give?

Question 1:   Answer 1:

Question 2:   Answer 2:

What is the King violently reacting against?

9. What crime does Esther repeat in 8:3-4?

How would you categorize this disobedience?

What usually accompanies such an act?

Were the Jews usually a disobedient people? Support your answer from the book of Esther.

What are you learning about Queen Esther?

What does the narrator value?

10. Think back to the beginning of the story. Why was it so unlikely Esther would rise to intervene in the annihilation of her people?

For what time and purpose have you been divinely appointed?

Is God asking you to take a risk?

What are the obstacles? The rewards?

Will you obey Him?

For Further Study
1. When is it right to disobey the Law? Determine your answer from Scripture.
2. What was the difference between Vashti's disobedience and that of Esther?
3. Consult a Bible atlas and locate Susa. Look up Esther, Ahasuerus, and Persia, noting any helpful information.

•TOOL CHEST•
(A Suggested Optional Resource)

BIBLE ATLAS
When we do a good Bible study we sometimes try to read a passage as if we were watching a movie, or better yet, as if we were there. We try to imagine the landscape, climate, architecture, utensils, and dress. Knowing these details can make the Scriptures come alive to us and refresh our Bible study. Before we travel we usually consult an atlas to note our route and any interesting facts about our destination. Many of us will never be so fortunate as to travel to Biblical lands. The editors of Bible atlases know this and seek to bring the lands of the Old and New Testaments to us. The next time you are in a church library visit the reference section and treat yourself to 20 minutes in a Bible atlas. You will find it fascinating!

Atlas of the Bible (Thomas Nelson Publishers)
The Moody Atlas of Bible Lands (Moody Press)
New Bible Atlas (Tyndale House Publishers)
The Westminster Historical Atlas to the Bible (The Westminster Press)

4

Living Right in a Wrong World

•FOOD FOR THOUGHT•

If we live rightly in a wrong world, sooner or later there will be conflict. Jesus' followers were described by some of their enemies as "the men who turned the world upside down" (Acts 17:6). Perhaps they should rather have been called "the men who turned the world right side up." Anyway, it's obvious you can't stand the world on its head or put it on its feet without a lot of people getting shaken up!

There is no doubt about it, we live in a "wrong" world. It wasn't always so. There was a day and age when everything was "all right," and nothing was wrong at all. But then Satan introduced sin into the universe and fathered the deepest of evil things. He demands our allegiance just as he demanded loyalty from Adam and Eve. He hates anyone who worships the Lord and continues to try to obliterate God's people.

Being a murderer from the beginning, Satan has not changed his character, objectives, or tactics. In fact, it is impossible for him to change because he is pure evil; he can't improve himself because pure evil desires to be nothing else. It should come as no surprise then that wrong people, living in a wrong world following the wrong leader tend to behave wrongly! They lend themselves unwittingly to do the work of the enemy of righteousness. Satan fosters wrong attitudes in people's minds, and one of his main plays is to fuel the fires of prejudice until they explode like dark clouds covering the sunlight of God's love.

It is easy to see who is behind the animosity toward God's children that, when fully developed, leads to genocide. It is a satanic scheme fleshed out in human drama. Cain murdered Abel; Moses was sought by Pharaoh's soldiers as they attempted to drastically limit the population growth of the people of Israel; the Edomites, Canaanites, and Agagites manifested their long hostility towards Judah and Israel. The source of such movements is surely the devil, out to thwart God's redemptive purposes. The historic outworking of all this diabolical animosity involves all God's people—Christians and Jews alike. Jesus Himself said, "If the world hates you, keep in mind that it hated Me first" (John 15:18). The final dramatic conflict to the death will be played out at the end of the age with the appearance of the anti-Christ.

Our own particular focus at this time is Haman and his amazing hatred for Israel. We are lent some light and understanding on the matter as we realize that Haman was an Agagite; a descendant of a group of people who had harbored a continuous hatred toward Israel. Haman was like an ancient Hitler.

Nine years passed since Xerxes deposed his rebellious queen, replacing her with the beautiful Esther. Mordecai and Esther thwarted a plot to kill the king by informing Xerxes. The plotters were summarily disposed of and the details carefully recorded in the King's records.

However, Haman was the one who was promoted to be Xerxes' prime minister rather than Mordecai who had just saved the king's life. It is at this point that conflicts arose between good and evil, between light and darkness. Haman the Agagite was about to give Esther and Mordecai the Jew the chance to live "rightly in a wrong world."

Having been promoted to such a position of influence, Haman began to demand the respect he felt was due him. In fact, he demanded a lot more than respect; he wanted groveling homage! He decided that everyone must bow down to him whenever he appeared. An edict enforcing this was signed by the king at Haman's request, and the signal went out to the four corners of the realm. Everyone began to bow down to Haman . . . except Mordecai the Jew! The issue here is Mordecai's Jewishness. After all, why wouldn't he bow down before the representatives of Xerxes? Others had bowed before him in similar situations without apparently compromising their faith. Mordecai probably refused to bow because Haman was a descendent of the king of the Amalakites who were among some of Israel's oldest and most bitter enemies (Ex. 17:8-15).

Now the plot began to pick up. Haman was absolutely furious at Mordecai's brave refusal to bow. He became so outrageously angry, nothing else would appease him but to get rid of Mordecai. Having discovered his rival belonged to his bitter enemy the Israelites, Haman desired to kill every single one of them as well! He cleverly gained the king's permission for his plan by subtly suggesting that the Israelites' laws differed from the laws of the Medes and Persians (Es. 3:8-10). The Torah indeed marks out the Jew from all other races on earth in this regard. But Haman went on to insinuate that the Israelites must therefore be disloyal since they could not possibly give whole hearted allegiance to the king! Xerxes, having been suitably manipulated to Haman's satisfaction, was led to comply with the death edict and the deed was done!

One application we can draw from this particular part of the narrative is the fact that our "Christlikeness" may mean that the modern believer will never be considered a modest, law abiding citizen by his neighbors. It's hard when people will not accept us as reasonable, responsible human beings just because we profess to believe in Christ. Someone has said we are called to endure this unjust judgment as a confessional or professional hazard.

Have you ever overheard yourself being described as a "holy roller," or a "Jesus freak"? Certainly most of us have been treated by our colleagues on some occasions as "odd balls" or "religious fanatics." I remember sitting before an empty dessert plate at a fashionable wedding reception as the hostess whipped away a plate of delicious trifle right from under my nose because, as she announced in a loud voice, "It has sherry in it, and you wouldn't want *that*, being as religious as you are!" However, these sorts of mild discomforts are very easy to live with compared to the dilemma that Mordecai's bold stand incurred. Though he had to face the consequences, we see Mordecai living his life under the principal, "Submit when you can and be loyal when you can; but when you can't, stand up and take the heat."

The problem for all of us is to know when to bow to Haman. When I became a believer, my friends expected me to continue with a manner of life that I knew was no longer acceptable to Christ. Sometimes I could go along with my friends, and sometimes I couldn't without compromising my faith. This caused an awful lot of grief all around. For one thing, I discovered it was not always crystal clear when it was right to bow to Haman and when it wasn't. Troubled about it, I asked Janet, the girl who had led me to faith in the Lord, to give me some guidelines. Basically she offered me three helpful ideas.

"First," she said, "I resist bowing down to Haman if it affects God. When the law of God contravenes the law of man, then that's the time to say no." We are told to obey the government that God in His permissive will has set over us (Rom. 13:1). But when that government tells us to contradict God's higher law, we must be subject to Him and realize its time to dig our heels in.

"My second guideline," Janet told me, "is to resist bowing down to Haman when it affects others." Mordecai was a leader who found himself put in a prominent visible position. We should expect right behavior from our leaders. People are watching us. The Jewish people were closely watching Mordecai in the king's palace. So what should he do? He obviously felt the time was right to show how the people of God do not submit to the wrong, but are willing to stand for the right.

My husband tells of his first assignment in a British bank when one day the manager told him to tell the customers he was out.

"Will you be out, sir?" Stuart nervously inquired.

"No, of course I won't," the man snapped, "But I don't want to be disturbed. Just do as I say and tell them I'm out!"

Stumbling over his words, 17-year-old Stuart said, "I'm sorry, sir, but I can't do that. And you should be glad. After all, if I told a lie *for* you, how would you ever know I wouldn't tell a lie *to* you?"

The time had come for young Stuart Briscoe to stand up and be counted. He would *not* bow down to Haman. People were watching, and Stuart felt he had a responsibility to God, to them, and to himself.

"My final guideline," Janet said, "is to resist bowing down to Haman when it affects myself." There is a spiritual principal here that we need to address. If our hearts do not condemn us, if we have clear consciences before God, and if no biblical laws are being contradicted, we can be submissive wives, loyal public servants, and effective employees. But we must be careful to live transparent lives before the Lord. Can God look into our hearts and see pure spirits, clean hands, right motives, and huge desires to do the right things whatever the consequences? If everything is spiritually in place in our lives, we will know when to bow to Haman, and when to stand up tall and straight for Jesus. As a friend of mine says, "If Jesus is first, you'll know what's next." If we bow when we ought not to, it will surely affect what we feel about ourselves and to have a clear conscience before God leads us to enjoy the best sense of self worth that I know! Haman can give us a pretty accurate picture of the self nature within us, striving to make us bow to the "old man" we used to serve without a thought, before we knew better. Paul said that sin and the old sin nature need not have dominion over us. Mordecai can be a picture of God's Spirit, giving us instructions about our behavior and reminding us that our God is able to help us as the challenges come along. And come they will, for there is much to be accomplished before the final curtain!

Haman I know;
He lives within me;
He is my worst self,
wanting to destroy
the spirit that
my God has lent me in
order to resist.

War is declared
early in a child's life.
I remember
listening to Haman and
doing what He told me
to do;
lying to my Mother, cheating at exams,
treating people in a shabby way.
O yes, Haman I know!

Haman intimidates me,
forcing me to cower,
demanding recognition,
wanting to be
served—
yea more—worshiped!

Haman must be faced
and overcome.
Mordecai will help me
not to capitulate.
Mordecai is like God's Spirit,
standing up straight and tall
with head erect,
Telling the truth, offering me
an example to follow,
showing the way,
helping me to overcome
evil.
O yes, Mordecai I know!

I am Esther, living for the King.

Haman is strong,
and I am weak.
But God is God!
Standing somewhere in
the shadows of my life,
He is ready to come
to my aid, if I ask Him to.
I will overcome someday—
If I take the risk.
Haman I know,
Mordecai I know,
I must strive to know
God best
of all!

•TALKING IT OVER•

1. REVIEW AND DISCUSS.   *10 minutes*

   Discuss some examples of modern-day anti-Semi-
   tism (for example, Russia's attitude toward Jews
   or snide, ethnic remarks).
   ☐ Who is behind all of this and why?
   ☐ Why did Mordecai refuse to bow to Haman
      when he was apparently content to bow to the
      king?

2. READ AND RESPOND.   *10 minutes*

   Read Romans 7:14-25 and 8:5-11. Discuss these
   passages.
   ☐ What do you learn about the flesh?
   ☐ What do you learn about the spirit?
   ☐ What do you learn about yourself?

3. REFLECT ON CARING.   *10 minutes*

   ☐ Do we really care about lost people?
   ☐ What do we need to do to care more?
   ☐ Share one thing that has helped you to care.

•PRAYING IT THROUGH•

Suggested Times

1. (As a group) Praise God for the freedom from persecution you enjoy. Pray for God's people living under persecution in foreign lands. Praise God for examples of Christians who "live in accordance with the Spirit" (Rom. 8:5).

5 minutes

2. (As a group) Pray for Christians who are bowing their knees to "Haman" or the "flesh." Pray for Christian leaders in this regard. Pray for the work of the Holy Spirit in believers' hearts.

5 minutes

3. (As a group) Praise God for those who cared about your soul and helped you spiritually. Pray for Christians to be awakened to a new need of prayer. Pray that believers will dare to take risks and be bold in their witnessing.

5 minutes

4. (On your own) Pray about the things God has taught you through this lesson.

5 minutes

•DIGGING DEEPER•

Mordecai

1. Mordecai is first introduced in Esther 2:5. What background information did the narrator think important to include about him?

   Name some famous Benjaminites in Biblical literature.

2. How would you describe the relationship between Esther and her uncle?

3. What kind of break seems to take place in chapter 2 between verses 18 and 19?

   What can you deduce about Mordecai from 2:19?

   Why is the phrase, "Mordecai was sitting at the king's gate," repeated, and what does it imply?

4. What does Mordecai's heroic act in 2:21-23 infer about his character? His loyalty to the king? His sentiments toward Persia?

5. If Mordecai was willing to risk his life to insure the king's safety, why would he refuse to kneel before and honor the king's noble?

6. How much time has elapsed between chapters 1 and 3?

7. Why would Haman want to go beyond murdering Mordecai to kill all the Jews living in Persia? What could account for such deep rooted hatred?

Does chapter 4 paint Mordecai as a law abiding citizen or as one who disregards the law?

Which are you?

8. In 4:4-17, Mordecai informs Esther of the king's edict. How could she have been ignorant of the decree?

Was it unfair of Mordecai to prod Esther so hard when he knew her consent to speak to Xerxes might very well mean sudden death?

Is there any doubt in Mordecai's mind that the king's command will be accomplished?

How does Mordecai respond to Queen Esther's obedience? (4:15-17)

9. What characteristics do you admire in Mordecai from 5:9?

Should Mordecai have refused to rise and kneel before Haman when his countrymen's lives were at stake?

Do you stick to what you believe is right, or do you often yield to pressure?

10. In chapter 6, how is it that Xerxes did not know that Mordecai the Jew had uncovered the plot and saved his life?

In chapter 6, Mordecai is finally rewarded for his loyalty to the king, and in chapter 8, for doing what he believed to be right in the eyes of God. What might result from your loyalty and obedience to your *King?* Is He seeking your loyalty and obedience on something?

11. Who is responsible for Mordecai's appointment? (8:1-2)

How did Mordecai use his influential position? (10:3)

Haman is pictured in Esther as whose enemy?

Mordecai is pictured as whose friend?

Both Esther and Mordecai were raised to royal positions for "such a time as this." Each traveled a difficult path to be used by God so mightily. Are you willing to go the same way?

Each possessed and practiced character traits which prepared them for grief and/or glory. Do you?

For Further Study
1. Memorize 4:14.
2. Read Esther again and circle all the repeating words, phrases, and ideas.
3. Look up *king's gate* or *gate* in James M. Feeman's *Manners and Customs of the Bible* (Bridge Publishing, Inc.) to find out what Mordecai was doing there.

•TOOL CHEST•
(A Suggested Optional Resource)

MANNERS AND CUSTOMS OF THE BIBLE

We are sometimes confused and sense we have not quite grasped the point when we come across ancient idioms or uncommon figures of speech in our Bible reading. A tool such as James M. Freeman's *Manners and Customs of the Bible* (Bridge Publishing, Inc.) can be of great assistance in deciphering unusual expressions. The three indexes to this book—analytical, textual, and topical—aid the Bible student in quickly discovering if the term or phrase he is curious about is discussed in Freeman's text. For example, if you were uncertain about the meaning of the words *eye of a needle* in Mark 10:25, you could look up Mark 10:25 in the textual index. Or you might discover *eye* in the topical index and find the definition easily accessible. This book comes in paperback and can be ordered through your local Christian bookstore.

5
Esther's Choice

•FOOD FOR THOUGHT•

Have you ever wondered what you would do if you found the cure for cancer? I'm sure you would share that secret with the world! But what would you do if you had cancer, and to share your secret might mean your cure might be taken away, putting your own life in jeopardy? Would you still share the precious truth you had discovered? Esther held in her hand the key to life for thousands of people who were doomed to die. On a certain day, Xerxes had agreed to a massacre of the Jews, and the deadly curse could not be averted or stopped, because no law of the Medes and Persians was ever reversed! Yet Queen Esther was a Jewess. She had been born into the nation of Israelites, and nothing could change her Jewishness. Therefore, along with thousands of her race, she faced extinction. Yet Esther had discovered a way out. With the help of Mordecai, she found a way to save herself and her people.

But herein lay her challenge. To keep the secret to herself and withhold information of her own nationality could save her own skin, while to share it could jeopardize everything. The questions are really very simple. How much did she care for other people? Did she care enough, dare enough, bear enough, and share enough with her world?

Esther brings us a vivid reminder of our own important choices. Those of us who are believers in Jesus have a very simple question to answer. Having found the cure for cancer of sin, that is, the knowledge of Christ who can save us, will we share our all important information with others who could eternally benefit? Having applied the "medicine" of salvation to our own sin sick souls, will we dispense it to others? Our choice mirrors that of the beautiful Esther. The problem is there are certain personal risks involved in sharing.

In some parts of the world today, there is the risk of the most ultimate kind. To share our faith in hostile territory may literally mean giving our life's blood. But for most of us the risk is far less life threatening, though cost there may be. We might suffer the loss of a relationship or lose face with friends. We may even find our jobs are in jeopardy. The challenge is this: Do we care enough, dare enough, bear enough, and share enough?

Shortly after I became a believer, I was faced with Esther's choice. I was teaching in Liverpool and found myself drawn into a youth work that involved activities out on the streets of the city late at night. Unchurched youngsters roamed around in groups with nothing to do but get into trouble. Many of these kids attended the school where I was teaching. Most of them came from home situations that had been disfunctional, and one could certainly conclude that not too many of them had had a chance to make it in life. But having come to Christ I knew that whether people came from good backgrounds or bad ones, all our hearts are "deceitful above all things and beyond cure" (Jer. 17:9). Christ is the cure for all of us; the answer to the problem of human sin. I was safe in Christ, but those children were not. Did I care?

As I struggled with the answer to that question, I heard a song. It's many years since I heard it, but the words went something like this:

> Do you know that souls are dying
> Do you care?
> Children lost and voices crying,
> Do you care?
> Can you say with God's dear Son
> Not my will but thine be done.
> Does it matter, does it matter
> Do you care?

I asked the Lord in that moment of time to touch my heart and help me to care enough to take action.

How much do we care? After all, once we have applied the death of Christ to our lives and have been saved, Jesus doesn't force us to do another thing from that moment to eternity. We are perfectly free to hug the precious secret of our "Christian" nationality to ourselves and let the world go to hell! What will motivate us to stick out our necks as Esther did and say, "If I perish, I perish!"? (Es. 4:16) My motivation then and now lies in the story of the grace of God. Jesus decided to share His secret of life with us by dying and saving us to make sure we had a means of defending ourselves against our deadly enemy, the Haman of our souls, Satan himself. How much our hearts are touched by what He did for us will surely determine how much we sacrifice for Him.

Mordecai certainly cared about people. He did everything possible to save the Jews. He declared his own nationality, stood up to Haman, and encouraged Esther to use her influence with the king. But it is to Esther, not Mordecai, we need to look at this particular point in the story. What did she do, and why did she do it? What motivated her to care enough, to dare enough, to bear enough, and to share enough?

Esther did not have a Gospel of John in her hand! She could not read the story of Christ, suffering according to the will of God on our behalf. But she opened her heart to the truth that she did know and allowed the Word of God to move her to do the right thing. Mordecai reminded her that God had a special job for His people to do and they needed to be preserved in order to do it. But Mordecai also reminded Esther that in the Lord's sovereign grace He allows us to cooperate in His plans. Why let someone else have the privilege of being the vehicle of light and life?

As we daily read the Scriptures, we, like Esther, can become motivated to be God's man or woman of the moment! We can align ourselves with His will and purposes and say, "Here am I—send me!" So the first thing that will motivate us will be an exposure to the Scriptures.

The second thing that will get us moving, will be to "hang around" the saints. Mordecai cared for others, and Esther found his compassion was catching! Try to make friends with people who are sold out for Christ and His cause; their characteristics will rub off on you.

Third, practice self denial. What's the best-dressed Christian person wearing today? Spiritual sackcloth, of course! I need to cultivate a humility of spirit that communicates the fact I will strip my life of all the trappings that clutter it up and give myself to God in a period of prayer and self denial, making me useful to Him. We all need to stay in God's presence long enough to honestly say, "OK, Lord, I'll do Your will—and if I perish, I perish!"

We need to ask ourselves the following questions: Does my own lifestyle so speak of self denial that others come to life? Do I care enough to dare enough to share enough about Jesus? Am I never more than a moment away from realizing that people are lost? Just what am I doing about it?

Prayer and fasting are close companions in the Scriptures. Without getting into a study of fasting, it's enough to say our prayers *must* be in earnest if they are to be heard. Fasting concentrates our energies and focuses our spiritual heart beat on the issue at hand. Sometimes, as Jesus said, "This kind can come out only by prayer" (Mark 9:29). Whether it be a demon-possessed child—a huge temptation that needs to be overcome—or a life-threatening situation, we need to practice both prayer and fasting. Jesus practiced them both. Should we do less? Only this way will Haman be mastered.

But we are such weak creatures. How much we need others to help us even in our self denial! With a great sense of her own inadequacy, Esther asked Mordecai to join her in her fast and called the nation of Israel to do the same. Not only did she ask for the support she would need from people she didn't even know, she called her own maidens to pray with her in a three day fast. Esther was surely in earnest! Note that the Bible says they drank no water for that period of time. But if you're going to care enough, you're going to have to bear enough before you'll find the courage to share enough to save lost people.

Will we pay the price as Esther did? Will we say with the Queen of Persia, "All right, Lord, whatever it is, I shall do it and if I perish in the doing, I perish"? The answer to that question may determine whether some human beings spend eternity in heaven or in hell!

•TALKING IT THROUGH•

1. READ AND REVIEW.   *10 minutes*
   Read chapter 4:1-17. Review the situation, Esther's dilemma, and Mordecai's request. Half the group should pretend they are Esther and half the group pretend they are Mordecai. Each group should say what they think should be done.

2. DISCUSS.   *10 minutes*
   Do we care enough?
   ☐ Discuss apathy and its causes. Why don't we care enough to share the gospel? Be as honest as you can.
   ☐ What has Esther "said" to you today?
   ☐ What has Mordecai taught you?
   ☐ How can the Scriptures play a part in motivating us to evangelize?
   ☐ How do we know which particular passages to study?

3. REFLECT.   *5 minutes*
   ☐ Who has been a "Mordecai" to you?
   ☐ Where can we meet with such inspiring people?
   ☐ What has sackcloth to do with sharing your faith?

4. PRAY.   *5 minutes*
   Pray about your own heart's need in response to this message.

•PRAYING IT THROUGH•

Suggested Times

---

1. (As a group) Praise God for all the people who care enough to share enough of the Gospel so that people can go to Heaven. Name some people. Be specific.

5 minutes

---

2. (As a group) Pray for:
   - ☐ an adequate discipleship program in your church so that the Scriptures may be faithfully taught.
   - ☐ the training of evangelists.
   - ☐ people dependent on a missionary taking them God's Word.

10 minutes

---

3. (On your own) Pray for yourself and for renewed vision and zeal.
   - ☐ Pray for a caring compassionate heart.
   - ☐ Pray you will learn to dress your spirit in sackcloth and practice the discipline of prayer and fasting.

5 minutes

• DIGGING DEEPER •

Haman

1. Why was Haman introduced in 3:1 immediately after the events of 2:21-23?

   What stark contrast does the text draw?

   The narrator thought it important to include what one item of information in his introduction of Haman?

   For what was Haman honored?

2. Why should Haman want to take such drastic measures against not only Mordecai, but all the Jews? (3:2-6)

   Read Exodus 17:8-16; Numbers 24:7, 20; and Deuteronomy 25:17-19. What else might account for Haman's exorbitant cruelty?

3. In Esther 3, Haman pitted himself against a man and a people that God is blessing and whom God has used for His purpose. Have you unjustly pitted yourself against someone God favors? What should you do about this?

4. Of what were the Jews guilty, according to Haman? (3:8)

Is there any crime in the fact that they were scattered or that they had different customs than the Persians?

What kind of merit was behind Haman's accusations?

How did he refer to the Jews?

5. What does the narrator personally feel about Haman? (3:10)

How did the citizens of Susa respond to Haman's decree?

What was the sentiment between the Jews and the Persians at this time?

Were the Jews in captivity to the Persians?

6. From 5:7-14, list some qualities of Haman's character.

7. An ironic twist develops in chapter 6. What picture of Haman stands in vivid contrast to 3:2 and 5:9?

How does the response of Haman's wife and advisors in 6:12-14 prepare the reader for the next scene?

Is Haman aware of Esther's nationality? How do you account for this?

Who turned out to be the king's real enemy in this story?

Do you ever take special privileges without asking permission first? Think of a few examples.

8. Where did Haman's prejudice lead him?

What picture of him do you again see in chapter 7?

The king mistook Haman's actions for rape. Why is this an accurate description of what Haman had attempted?

9. The plot against the Jews was reversed by the king's second edict. Why does the narrator place so much emphasis on the Jews' moderation in 9:10, 16?

Read 1 Samuel 15. Saul, a Benjamite like Mordecai, committed what sin? What were the results?

Why do you think the narrator points out that Haman was an Amalekite, a descendant of King Agag?

What sin of Saul's were the Jews in Esther redressing?

10. Why did Haman's plot not materialize?

Are you scheming any plots, deals, or situations for which you need to repent?

Do you need to right any wrongs you have committed? Why not take time to ask the Lord for help to right your wrongs.

For Further Study
1. Skim the dialogues different people have with Xerxes and notice how they address him. Study Esther 3:8. What is different about the way Haman addressed the king? Haman may have sought to assume a level of intimacy with the king that was inappropriate. Are any of your relationships marked by an inappropriate intimacy? Do you try to be too familiar with people in the limelight?

•TOOL CHEST•
(A Suggested Optional Resource)

TODAY'S HANDBOOK OF BIBLE CHARACTERS
This creative resource produced by Bethany House Publishers walks the reader book by book and many times chapter by chapter through the Old and New Testaments introducing him/her to the corresponding Bible characters. Seven hundred and forty biblical characters come to life as E.M. Blaiklock condenses the Bible material to present a brief biographical sketch on each. Both man's depravity and his spiritual sensitivity are shown in the lives of these men and women who sometimes wrestled, sometimes failed, and sometimes pleased God. The lessons they learned firsthand can be our own if we acquaint ourselves with their lives and character. You will want to compare your character studies of Xerxes, Esther, Mordecai, and Haman with those found in this text.

6
Doing Without the Courage

•FOOD FOR THOUGHT•

Very big decisions require a very big God to help us make them. Esther knew such a God. Jehovah was to prove to be as big as His name and as good as His Word. No big decisions should be made or no great changes should be undertaken without much personal prayer. Are you considering a career change, a relocation for your family, or a decision to marry? Then make very sure the whole project is bathed in prayer.

If others close to you and the situation can also be invited to pray, so much the better. Jesus Himself said, "If two of you on earth agree about anything you ask for, it will be done for you by My Father in heaven" (Matt. 18:19). Fasting and praying for three days gave Esther a chance to hear the voice of God. I'm quite sure she agonized over her decision to enter the king's presence and present her request because it was against the law. Sometime in the day or night of that vigil, God confirmed her course of action, and she emerged confident of at least one thing—she must go to the king and plead for her life and the lives of her people.

No big decision should be made without such careful preparation. Before Esther ever dressed herself in royal robes, she dressed her spirit in royal requests. Often people come to me and tell me of complicated situations that need remedying. After hours of talking, there seems to be no light on the issues. I have learned to advise a period of prayer and fasting that understanding may be given, love may be experienced, and hope and strength be gained for whatever actions must eventually be taken. It's amazing what a difference God can make in our lives and circumstances if we but give Him half a chance.

Where do you go for courage? Courage is a very scarce commodity. I have observed that there are not too many naturally courageous people around this planet. One tends to think of "God's greats" as men and women of immense courage, and yet even a cursory glance at the Scriptures convinces us otherwise. What an encouragement it was to me (a naturally fearful person) to discover that many of God's biggest and best servants were ordinary people full of fears and frights, panic and cries of help for their desperate plights. After Moses' death, Joshua, a man I envisioned as a virtual giant killer, found himself faced with a formidable task. First of all, he had to replace Moses! Now that surely was enough to frighten anyone out of his sandals. Then he was told he was to tackle nations of giants— not just one or two, but whole tribes of them! With his feet poised on the boundary lines of the Promised Land and his knees knocking, he turned to God in great trepidation. God answered his prayers saying, "Be strong and courageous. Do not be terrified; do not be discouraged, for the Lord your God will be with you wherever you go" (Josh. 1:9).

Have you ever been afraid of someone's face? What a giant that can turn out to be! As a preacher's wife, I have often feared an angry face in the foyer! *What have I done or said,* I wonder as the face flits past me intent on letting me see the set mouth and contemptuous glance. Sometimes it takes more strength to face a face, than face a foe like Xerxes, though I'm sure Esther was very much afraid of both Xerxes and his fearful face!

To confront anger, disapproval, or downright hostility requires a courage that God will surely give us if we will only ask Him. Joshua experienced God's strengthening words and inner power as He fought his giants. So did Esther as she faced her husband, and so will you and I, if we admit our lack of strength and turn to the One who stands in the shadows waiting to strengthen us!

(One of the first things we need to learn about courage is that it is in very short supply.) We need to admit our own drastic lack of it. Why it takes so many of us so long to admit that fact I will never know. Perhaps it has to do with human pride and the "old man" in us insisting he can do quite well against the giants without God!

(It is also good to remember that even our enemies are as bereft of courage as we are!) Everyone is frightened of something! The bravest man on the battlefield could well be a coward at home. Some kids are frightened of their parents while those same parents are frightened of their kids! Some people are scared silly of the family get-together at Christmas more than an air raid in the war. Others fear mice not men, day not night, or even their own daydreams never mind their nightmares. It's funny what giant fears have to be faced and overcome. But it's not very funny to have to overcome them! Having learned that courage to overcome our fears is in such short supply and that we are not alone in this respect, we must decide next that courage must not dictate action. If courage dictates our actions, it stands to reason that if there's not much courage, there won't be much action. Therefore, we all need to learn to live our lives on another set of principles altogether. In other words, if we only do and dare when we have the courage to do or dare, very little doing or daring will be done! We all need to practice the principle of faith.

Faith is doing something without the courage. Faith trusts God as we do something courageous without wanting to! Faith says, "It shall be done—look out devil here we come, God and I!" Faith is a very practical thing. It enlists our minds and helps us to believe that we were born for a purpose. There should be a sense of destiny born in upon us that says I was created for "such a time as this" (Es. 4:14). We must come to believe that we are the only ones who can serve the Lord in quite this way. In the words of a well known hymn, "There's a work for Jesus only you can do." The mind will need to be enlisted to believe this before faith can instruct the body to action.

The mind also needs to stop playing so many horror movies for our entertainment! The awful scenarios our fertile minds conjure up have to be experienced to be believed. The mind always seems to present us with the very worst possibilities about a certain course of action in graphic scenes and in glorious technicolor. There is one good thing—and only one good thing about watching such "mind movies." It is such a relief when none of the dreaded things you envisage happen. What joy to discover it was only a "mind movie" after all. If you are a negative person like I am, the practice of faith will be all the more necessary. I have found it a help to allow myself to think a little bit about the very worst things that could possibly happen to me. Even for a Christian I suppose death must be one of the worst experiences. But faith turns the movie off and points its finger to the Scriptures that tell me, "For me, to live is Christ and to die is gain" (Phil. 1:21). So even the worst thing I can think of can become the gateway into the best blessings. After all mind movies can bring me positive pictures as well.

Mind movies
need to be monitored
by Jesus.

He needs to set the
ratings for us.
D.G. stands for divine guidance,
and care should be taken
to ask for such
expert help
before such movies are
watched.
Movies with a L.M. rating are the best.
That stands for "love movies,"
beautiful pictures of
whatsoever things are
good, pure, honest, and true.
Jesus will watch such movies
with us.
He writes, directs, and
enjoys such positive fare Himself.
Yes, mind movies need to be monitored by Jesus!

Esther undoubtedly expected the worst to happen to her, but I'm sure prayer helped her to be as positive as possible under the circumstances. No one usually survived such a violation of Persian law as she was planning. And so she dressed in her lovely robes and stood trembling in the outer court waiting for an almost certain death sentence. I'm sure she tried to play some good mind movies! After all, the king had not called for her for over a month so she presumed she was thoroughly out of favor. But wonder of wonders, the worst did not happen. Out came the golden scepter to save her. What unutterable relief Esther must have felt when she touched the top of it. Mercy had won the day!

I once stood trembling outside a dance hall willing myself inside. I was convinced that if I ever got in, I would be humiliated, thrown out, or even physically assaulted. I wanted to ask the manager for permission to speak about Christ to the hundreds of young people that congregated there. My mind movie imagined the worst. But then I enlisted my mind for a more noble enterprise—I thought about the fact that those young folk needed Christ, and I had what they needed. I couldn't see too many people lined up outside that dance hall to tell them about Him. "For such a time as this" I had been born, and I knew it. The problem was that the courage I needed was conspicuous by its absence. But in that fearful moment, I trusted God to go with me. I went into that place without the courage, but I went in with God!

Faith believes Him when He says ". . . and lo, I am with you always, even unto the end of the age." It doesn't say lo, the "courage" is with you, but rather, lo, "I" am with you always even unto the end of the age even when the courage isn't! (Matt. 28:20) So I enlisted my mind to believe that and my will to move my body forward and I found myself inside that dance hall incredibly able to take charge! I asked to see the manager (my Xerxes), and lo and behold he held out his golden scepter to me—he asked me what I wanted. When I told him, he granted me permission to speak to the kids about Christ. What joy and what lessons I learned.

Faith gives us help to go where He tells us to go with no certainty that Xerxes will hold out that golden scepter! Sometimes he will and sometimes he won't, however hard we've prayed about it. The point is that we are to be obedient because, at that moment, obedience is all that matters. Our greatest determination must be to follow Jesus, take up our cross, do the will of God because it must be done, and do it with all our might as if the world depends on it. Esther found courage after obedience and so shall we. Like Esther, we must not allow courage to dictate our actions, but rather let Christ direct us wherever He wants.

•TALKING IT THROUGH•

Suggested Times

1. READ AND DISCUSS.   *15 minutes*
   After reading the following verses, discuss prayer
   and fasting.

Scripture	Reasons	Who fasted?	How long?	Results?
2 Sam. 1	Saul's death	David & his men	all day	had Amalekite killed
2 Sam. 11–12	for his son's life	David	7 days	son died
1 Kings 21	Naboth's vineyard	Naboth's city	1 day	Naboth was stoned
Neh. 1	Jerusalem had fallen	Nehemiah	some days	prayed for redemption
Jer. 36:6	people were wicked	all of Jerusalem	a day	
Dan. 6:18	Daniel in lions den	King Darius	night	Daniel spared
Ps. 35:13		David	a time	unanswered prayer

2. SHARE.   *15 minutes*
   ☑ Of what are you fearful?
   ☑ Discuss your fears of witnessing.
   ☑ Read Psalm 27 together. Which verse did you
      like most?
   ☑ Share an experience when you have been obe-
      dient in faith without courage. How did it turn
      out?

81

•PRAYING IT THROUGH•

Suggested Times

1. (On your own) Praise God for: *5 minutes*
   - ☐ an "Esther" you know.
   - ☐ prayer warriors or prayer partners.
   - ☐ answered prayer.

2. (On your own) Pray for: *5 minutes*
   - ☐ "negative" people to use faith as a positive tool.
   - ☐ people plagued with fears.
   - ☐ people to act in faith without the courage.

3. (As a group) Pray for men and women who have power to be merciful in: *5 minutes*
   - ☐ the work place
   - ☐ the home
   - ☐ the mission field
   - ☐ the church
   - ☐ the courts
   - ☐ the White House

4. Think about what you have learned about fasting. Pray about some of these things together. Silently promise God you will fast and pray about a special need. Keep your promise!   *5 minutes*

•DIGGING DEEPER•

Royalty

1. The book of Esther was either written during the exile of the Jews or shortly after. Think about what you know of foreign invasion, occupation, and deportation. What were some of the adversities and circumstances facing those who lived during Queen Esther's time?

2. The words *king, queen, royalty, power, dominion,* and *kingdom* are all derived from the same Hebrew stem. How many times do these derivatives appear in the book? What might so many occurrences imply?

3. Is King Xerxes the only monarch mentioned?

   Are royalty and royal power applied only to monarchy? If not, who else do they modify?

   Skim chapters 1–2. Does the word *royal* ever stand alone? What objects or qualities does it modify?

   Vashti is not the ruling monarch, yet she does have royal power. What do 1:19 and 2:17 suggest about Esther?

4. When does Esther first use her royal privilege? How often does she make use of her power? How does she feel about using it? Does her attitude change?

Chart the number of instances Esther employs her royal position and prerogative. One example is given for you.

Reference	*Instance*
4:5	Esther summons and orders Hathach to inquire of Mordecai.

Chart the various responses to Esther's prerogatives.

Hathach 4:6

4:9

Mordecai 4:15

Maids 4:16

Xerxes 5:3

What do these responses indicate?

How is Esther's royal power and influence shown to be higher than Xerxes? (8:8)

5. The theme of royalty is very prominent in chapter 6. What transfer of royalty is foreshadowed?

What is the narrator suggesting by emphasizing 2:17 and 6:8?

6. What difference do you observe in Mordecai's apparel between 6:8 and 8:15?

How do the non-Jewish citizens of Susa respond to Mordecai's position?

What detail did the narrator include in his introduction of Mordecai that contributes to this theme?

From your earlier lessons, what was one reason Saul's kingship was removed from him? How does the narrator validate Mordecai's kingship?

Although Mordecai is presented as a king, does he pose a threat to Xerxes?

7. What might these royal pictures have suggested to a Jewish audience under foreign rule?

Were they meant to encourage the Jews to rebel against Persia?

8. The Jew's estimation of themselves was probably very poor at the time Esther was written. Yet, the Book of Esther depicted them as a valuable and royal people whom God was shielding from opposition for His purposes. Do you have a low estimation of yourself? Are you confronted with overwhelming and adverse circumstances? What is God's message to you from Esther today? On what does He want you to focus your attention?

For Further Study
1. Read the introduction to Joyce Baldwin's commentary, *Esther*, published by InterVarsity Press. Also, read the portions of her commentary which pertain to the questions and difficulties you have discovered in your study. Do you agree with her conclusions? Why or why not?

•TOOL CHEST•
(A Suggested Optional Resource)

COMMENTARIES
Bible commentaries should be consulted after you have thoroughly studied a passage of Scripture yourself. They are excellent resources and should supplement your personal study, not replace it. Commentaries provide a good check and balance for inductive study. You can compare your conclusions with those of noted Bible scholars, but always bear in mind the best answer is the one supported by Scripture and which best fits the context.

In choosing a commentary, make sure that you understand the author's theological persuasion. This does not mean to always avoid less conservative works, but be aware of and cautious of more liberal presuppositions. A few commentaries on Esther to consult are:

Esther by Joyce Baldwin (InterVarsity Press)
Ezra, Nehemiah, Esther by D.J. Clines (Eerdmans)
Esther, The Triumph of God's Sovereignty by John C. Whitcomb, Jr. (Moody Press)

7
The Person God Uses

•FOOD FOR THOUGHT•

What a releasing thing it is to discover that courage is doing the right thing without the courage. One such reckless action leads to a huge sense of dependence which results in us proving God's worth.

"He was there all the time," exclaimed a young girl who dared to tell her wild bunch of friends about her Saviour. "He came through," confirmed an elderly lady recently released from the hospital after major surgery. "If I don't walk on 'risk's edge,' I will never know I can trust Him," confided a young boy struggling with a big decision to go to the mission field.

If you never risk, you never depend. And if you never depend, you never prove He's there! I remember our three small children jumping off a high wall into their father's waiting arms. "Jump!" shouted Dad. Without any hesitation they jumped. This was their daddy and they trusted him. It was safe to take the risk.

Those of us who are timid where sharing our faith is concerned need to practice risk-taking as a regular discipline. Perhaps we can offer our help to the pastor, telling him we'll have a go at any job that needs doing that no one else will do! That's a risk where we can learn to depend in a hurry.

Once a risk is taken and God has proven faithful, the next risk doesn't look quite so hard! Look at Esther. The first huge risk over, she had the chance to clinch the thing. But she didn't. Having been asked by the king to state her request, she invited Haman and the king to a banquet. At the banquet, her husband requested a second time that she tell him what she wanted, but again Esther procrastinated, inviting them both to yet another banquet the following day! She certainly took another huge risk doing that. Xerxes could have had a bad night (which, in fact, he did!) resulting in a terrible mood the following day. However, one gets the impression that the second risk was easier for Esther than the first one. And so it is that faith grows faith as faith grows! And faith needs risks' soil in order to flourish.

The very first time I opened my mouth to witness for Christ I lost a friend. It took an enormous amount of courage. It was a risk, but a risk I felt I had to take. Daring to dare, I told my best friend in a faltering voice that I had become a believer during my brief stay in the hospital. She did not hold out the golden scepter. She responded by ending our relationship! Even after the bad experience I had just had, it did not take nearly so much effort to risk witnessing a second time to another close friend. I found faith grows faith because faith trusts God to enable us to do the right thing in a wrong world.

The person God uses is a person who has stopped giving God conditions for his obedience. The only golden scepter any of us should be interested in, is the one held out to us in heaven when we finally approach the eternal throne. All of us can be assured of that one!

The people God uses are like Esther and Mordecai, not Vashti and Haman. An obedient follower, a broken servant! "God chose the foolish things of the world to shame the wise; God chose the weak things of the world to shame the strong" (1 Cor. 1:27).

I have a beautiful cut glass vase. I often put beautiful roses in it. When I do that, visitors who see it usually comment, "What a beautiful vase, and what pretty flowers you've put in it." I also have a pot. It's old and has been broken once. When I put roses in it no one says, "What a lovely pot," but simply gasp at the beauty of the flowers.

That is why God uses the weak to confound the wise. An Esther instead of a Vashti, a Mordecai instead of a Haman. He does it in order that "no one may boast before Him" (1 Cor. 1:29).

Esther was truly a broken vessel. She had been broken by her past and present circumstances and having been broken, the light shone through her life. She reminds me very much of the story of Gideon. Gideon had been threshing wheat in a winepress. He was frightened of the Midianites who were plundering Israel's crops. God appeared to him and addressed him as a "mighty warrior" (Jud. 6:12). I'm sure the angel of the Lord had his tongue in His cheek to greet him in such a way. He then soothed Gideon's fears and coaxed him into daring to dare. Gideon ended up routing the Midianites with a simple but very clever ruse. With a mere handful of 300 men, he surrounded the camp of the Midianites and, at an appropriate time, blew trumpets and broke the vessels that contained lamps. Waking from their sleep, the Midianites saw the circle of lights, thought they were overwhelmed by superior forces, panicked, and fled. The broken vessels had sent light into the darkness dispelling the enemy. I cannot help but wonder if Paul had this story in mind when he wrote, "For God, who said, 'Let light shine out of darkness,' made His light shine in our hearts to give us the light of the knowledge of the glory of God in the face of Christ. But we have this treasure in jars of clay to show that this all-surpassing power is from God and not from us" (2 Cor. 4:6-7)

Esther, herself a broken vessel, thought of an especially ingenious ruse to route her own particular band of Midianites, namely Haman and his cohorts. Esther, passing her supreme test, displayed not only courage but cleverness. As we read on in the story of Esther we see a resolute use of all of her resources. After all, shining was a dangerous business in that particularly dark sky. Imagine the challenge she faced. The men in this woman's life were no weak-willed willies! Xerxes and Haman together formed a formidable team of terror. But God in us is equal. Esther had to overcome her own fears and attempt to solve the complex problem of how to reverse a law that was not reversible. Using a mixture of flattery and coyness, she got exactly what she wanted—another banquet on another day, and then she was ready! She needed time to set Haman up. After all, he was the king's favorite and to accuse him too hurriedly could have undone all her plans. Esther must have felt terribly weak and vulnerable. But obedience and a willingness for God to use her won the day.

Now the story takes a most dramatic turn. That very night Xerxes could not sleep. When I cannot sleep, I usually turn on a light and read a book. Things haven't changed much since the days of Xerxes. And so it was that the king called for his servants to bring him a book to read.

Lying propped up on his pillows, the king read the book and, to his great surprise, discovered a piece of information that reminded him of something he had forgotten all about. His servant Mordecai had saved his life, and he had never rewarded him! The king read on into the early hours of the morning.

Meanwhile, on the other side of town, Haman was having trouble sleeping as well. He had excitedly boasted to Zeresh his wife and to his friends that he alone had been invited to eat with the king and queen that very day. However, the sight of Mordecai his bitter foe sitting firmly in place when he passed by instead of groveling at his feet, had robbed him of all his privileged pleasure. Zeresh, apparently well suited to be Haman's mate, suggested Haman spend his evening building a gallows suitable for Mordecai's neck. The idea of watching Mordecai's corpse swinging merrily in the breeze obviously appealed to Haman and he got to work. Rising early he arrived eagerly at the palace just at the time King Xerxes was wondering how he could reward Mordecai. Xerxes asked Haman what he would do for the man the king delighted to honor. Quite naturally, Haman thought to himself, *Who would the king delight to honor but me?* He quickly suggested that the man in question should be put on the king's own horse and paraded through the streets with a herald proclaiming before him, "This is what is done for the man the king delights to honor" (Es. 6:9). "Go at once," said the king, "and do it for Mordecai the Jew."

"How are the mighty fallen!" God in the shadows is fitting the pieces of the jigsaw puzzle all together.

Esther, sleeping, perhaps fitfully, had no idea that she and God were well on the way to seeing the end of Haman the great Jew-hater.

Nothing but nothing happens by happenstance. Not for the child of God in the center of the will of God. Man needs to look above for his answers, and see the individual footsteps of the obedient believer fit perfectly onto the pages of the story of God's dealings with mankind. We must be faithful and do our part, knowing with all certainty He will certainly do His!

•TALKING IT THROUGH•

Suggested
Times

---

1. READ AND DISCUSS.
   Read chapter 6 of the Book of Esther. Discuss the
   heavenly irony of the story.
   ☐ What do you like most about it?
   ☐ How is this story similar to the story of Ruth
   and Boaz?

10 minutes

---

2. READ AND DISCUSS.
   Read Psalm 73.
   ☐ What does it teach about the righteous?
   ☐ What does it teach about the wicked?
   ☐ Which verse from this Psalm would have
   helped Esther?

10 minutes

---

3. REVIEW.
   Review Hebrews 11:32-38.
   ☐ Who experienced the Golden Scepter?
   ☐ Who didn't?
   ☐ What conclusions do you draw?

10 minutes

•PRAYING IT THROUGH•

Suggested Times

---

1. (With a partner) Meditate on Psalm 73.
   □ Praise God for all the things Psalm 73 teaches you about Him.
   □ Pray for the wicked.

5 minutes

---

2. (As a group) List a few countries in the world that seem to be dominated by Xerxes-like characters with "Haman" close at hand.
   □ Pray for the leaders of these countries.
   □ Pray for the believers living there.
   □ Pray for missionary endeavors.
   □ Pray that God will intervene.

10 minutes

---

3. (In twos) Quietly think of a frightening situation in your own life. How does Esther's example help you face it? If appropriate, share your need with your partner. Pray for each other.

5 minutes

•DIGGING DEEPER•

The Humble Are Exalted

1. Scripture repeatedly declares the unchampioned principle, "For whoever exalts himself will be humbled, and whoever humbles himself will be exalted" (Matt. 23:12). From your study of the following passages, what blessings will those who humble themselves receive?
   ☐ Psalm 18:27
   ☐ Psalm 25:9
   ☐ Psalm 149:4
   ☐ Proverbs 3:34
   ☐ Proverbs 11:2
   ☐ Proverbs 15:33
   ☐ Isaiah 66:2
   ☐ Luke 14:11
   ☐ Luke 18:14
   ☐ James 4:6

   What do many of these verses teach about the man or woman who exalts themselves?

2. From your study of the following verses, is humility just a good idea for the believer to exercise?
   ☐ Zephaniah 2:3
   ☐ Ephesians 4:2
   ☐ Philippians 2:3
   ☐ Titus 3:2
   ☐ James 4:10
   ☐ 1 Peter 5:6

   Is the lack of humility a lesser sin than any other?

3. In what ways did Esther humble herself?

How did Mordecai practice humility?

Does the fact that Mordecai refused to bow to Haman refute that he practiced humility?

4. Describe someone you know who exemplifies humility. How did they develop this Christian virtue?

5. What does the world teach/model regarding humility?

6. Do you have a problem with self-exaltation? Recall the last time you tried to make yourself look good to others. Why did you do so? What do you need to do about this sin?

7. Look up the word *proud* in a concordance and also several of its occurrences. What does the Bible teach about the proud?

Do you struggle with pride? How has your pride troubled you or been hurt today? Confess, ask for God's forgiveness and His grace to combat the ugly sin of pride.

8. Esther is full of subtle contrasts which illustrate the humble being exalted above the proud. Identify a few.

9. Is Romans 12:16 true of you? It was of Queen Esther. Examine your heart and ask the Lord to show you how you can begin to implement these words in your own life today.

At the end of the week, list the opportunities God gave you this week to live out this verse and how you responded.

For Further Study
1. Memorize Matthew 23:12 with a friend.
2. Make a list of other Bible characters who learned this lesson. Study their lives and ask how they grew, what obstacles they overcame, and what benefits they received from their obedience to Scripture.

•TOOL CHEST•
(A Suggested Optional Resource)

KNIGHT'S TREASURY OF ILLUSTRATIONS
This fascinating book produced by Eerdmans is filled with delightful and thought-provoking quotations and anecdotes to illustrate Bible truths. You simply look under the table of contents for the subject you are interested in and turn to the page listed. There you will find several pages of pointed and meaningful illustrations to help bring home Scriptural principles.

8
The Daystar

•FOOD FOR THOUGHT•

What a feeling of satisfaction it gives us to see Haman rushing home with his tail between his legs? It must have been a humiliating experience to walk in front of the king's horse leading Mordecai through cheering crowds declaring, "This is what is done for the man the king delights to honor" (Es. 6:11). How could Haman ever face his colleagues again?

Zeresh his wife was there to greet him along with his family and friends, but they were very little help. "Since Mordecai, before whom your downfall has started, is of Jewish origin, you cannot stand against him—you will surely come to ruin!" they said to him (Es. 6:13). Almost at once, officials from the royal palace arrived to escort him to Esther's banquet. I can imagine Zeresh saying to her husband, as he hurriedly left his home, "Perhaps the queen will restore you to favor."

The queen, however, as we well know had something very different indeed in mind! With the banquet well under way, Xerxes must have been very curious about Esther's reason for risking her life to enter his presence without an invitation. Feeling in a generous mood, he promised to grant her request, up to the half of his kingdom! (Es. 7:2)

Esther, her heart beating furiously, cast herself down at the king's feet and pleaded for her life and the life of her people. The king was absolutely astonished.

"Where is the man who has dared to do such a thing?" he asked in fury (Es. 7:5). Now was Esther's finest hour, perhaps the most dramatic moment of her life. Pointing to Haman who must have been totally flabbergasted, the queen declared, "The adversary and enemy is this vile Haman" (Es. 7:6).

The king was beside himself. He stormed into the garden in a fit which left Esther alone with Haman. What happened next is a little difficult to fathom. Haman, realizing this was the end for him, threw himself down by the side—or onto—the couch on which the queen was reclining and begged for mercy. However, verse 8 of chapter 7, leads us to believe that Haman in some way made a pass at the queen. It may well be that Esther so arranged herself on the couch it just appeared that way to Xerxes. We really don't know. What we do know, however, is that Xerxes returned from the courtyard and saw what he thought was an attempted sexual attack on his beautiful wife!

At this, the king's servants, covered Haman's face with the death mask, and suggested to Xerxes that a fitting solution would be to put the gallows Haman had built for Mordecai to good use! "Hang him on it!" the king ordered at once—and so they did, and perfect justice was done! (Es. 7:9-10)

An amazing second time Esther stepped into the throne room. This time she was a little more sure of her reception. The golden scepter was extended, and she, having elevated Mordecai into a position of influence, presented their joint request that another irreversible law be introduced to counter the first edict. She suggested that on the same day of the irreversible order to attack and plunder the Jews, her people be allowed to take up whatever means they have at their disposal to defend themselves. This request was granted, and the order went out to tell the Jews to get ready. When the day finally arrived, the Israelites took a terrible revenge on their foes, effectively putting an end to their opposition throughout the kingdom (Es. 9:5).

Many questions have been raised concerning the final chapters of the book of Esther. Even King Xerxes himself, no novice in the matter of killing, raised his royal eyebrows at the number of people the Jews killed within his own royal city of Susa (Es. 9:12). Even though deliverance had been granted to God's people, they still had to fight for it. Apparently there were enough of Haman's friends and cohorts around to still pose a threat to the Israelites and even to Esther herself. Commentaries point out that we are reading an act of self defense only, and that the people of God took no plunder at all from the people they fought (Es. 9:9).

The last chapter of Esther describes the establishment of the feast of Purim where God's people would be reminded regularly of the great deliverance that God had brought about on their behalf. The story ends with God's stars, Esther and Mordecai, burning brightly, bringing glory to God, and making it a little easier for dimmer stars to do their part in the Persian sky.

Let's review the lessons we have learned. First, Haman could *never* have succeeded against Mordecai. God would not have permitted it. The permissive will of God comforts us with the knowledge that God holds all the cards and the end of the game is well known to Him.

Second, the fact that God stands in the shadows does not mean He is in any way inactive; it simply means we cannot always see His face clearly. But then Jesus Himself said, "Blessed are those who have not seen and yet have believed" (John 21:29).

Third, faith speaks of the reality of unseen things and causes us to base everything on facts of faith revealed to us from the Scriptures. To be tuned into what God is doing is essential, and it is in the Bible that the big plan is explained. And what is the big plan? The big plan is concerned with the Daystar—Jesus Christ, who 2,000 years ago was hung up against a dark noonday sky upon a cross of wood. The Daystar though dimmed by the darkness of our sin can never be obliterated as Satan intended Him to be. The darkness cannot overcome the Light (John 1:5).

Fourth, all other stars pale in significance beside Jesus in all His glory. They simply point to the cross and to Him who is the Light of the world.

Fifth, it is our turn. Those of us who believe in the Light are called to be His witnesses. "Those who are wise will shine like the brightness of the heavens, and those who lead many to righteousness, like the stars for ever and ever" (Dan. 12:3).

Our high and holy calling is to hang high and shine brightly, reflecting the light of our Daystar. Jesus Christ is our Lord, and we would hope others would live a life of righteousness because of our witness.

The Morning Star was thought by ancient people to be the planet Venus. It always preceded the sun and shone in the early morning. It brought hope of a new day and a new page of history in the making.

When Jesus Christ became the Light of my life, He became my Daystar. He is the brightest spot in my world and the bringer of good tidings. He is the light of my eyes and the love of my life; the giver of energy and the inspirer of dreams. Morning by morning, I enjoy my own personal spiritual feast of Purim by remembering the great deliverance He wrought for me when he fought Satan on my behalf and perished in hell that I may go to heaven. Yes, Jesus is my Daystar. How He longs to hear us say, "O dear Lord, here I am.

Hang me high wherever, whenever, however you wish!"

Daystar shining in my darkness
Daystar dawning in my heart
Daystar brighter than the sunlight
Jesus Christ thou art!
Daystar visiting my gloomy life
Daystar lighting up my years
Daystar pointing me to God above
Banishing my fears.
Daystar baby yet the ancient one,
Daystar God in Jewish frame,
Daystar journeying from eternity
For my sake you came.
Daystar shaped like cross of Christ for me
Daystar dying star of love
Daystar ensuring by thine agony
That I might shine above.

Finally, may we never forget—all stars are made by God; all stars are made to shine; and STARS SHINE BEST IN A DARK SKY!

• TALKING IT THROUGH •

Suggested Time

---

1. READ AND RECORD.   *15 minutes*
   Read Esther 6–8 right through without stopping.
   ☐ Write down one comment and one question.
   ☐ Share your findings with the group. Help each other with answers to the questions.

---

2. DISCUSS.   *5 minutes*
   Imagine yourself talking to a new Christian. You are trying to get her to read the book of Esther. What arguments would you use to persuade her?

---

3. READ AND REFLECT.   *10 minutes*
   Read the following verses and determine what each says to you.
   ☐ Numbers 24:17·
   ☐ Matthew 2:2
   ☐ 2 Peter 1:19 *light in dark*
   ☐ Philippians 2:15 *" in you shine "*
   ☐ Revelation 2:28 *26-28*
   ☐ Revelation 22:16

•PRAYER•

1. (As a group) Think about the cast of characters in this book.

   Vashti   Xerxes   Memucan Mordecai
   Esther   Haman   Zeresh

   ☐ What have you learned from each of these people? Pray about it.

   5 minutes

2. (As a group) Notice that the last chapters of Esther are full of violence. Pray for people caught up in:
   ☐ National violence
   ☐ Domestic violence
   ☐ Spiritual violence

   5 minutes

3. (In twos) Think about Jesus being the Bright Morning Star.
   ☐ Praise Him for being your Daystar.
   ☐ Pray that you may shine in your dark world and turn many to righteousness.

   5 minutes

4. (As a group) Pray as the Spirit leads you.

   5 minutes

•DIGGING DEEPER•

Good Triumphs Over Evil
1. Review your lessons and list the themes you have discovered in Esther.

How does the book present the activity of God in human affairs?

Where do you observe divine intervention? For example, how would you have expected Esther to have been treated in a foreign court? How did she earn Hegai's favor? Who ultimately chose Esther to be the Queen of Persia?

2. Number the coincidences in this story.

List the reversals.

To what do they point?

Yet, why is God's name absent from the entire book?

3. The narrator's point of view is that God's activity extends to what human structures?

Do you believe God is active in the realm we term as secular?

Is anything secular to God?

4. Does anything happen by chance in Esther?

Are there any coincidences in life?

What do you believe in regard to chance and coincidence in your own life? Does Scripture agree?

5. How does this story contribute to the Biblical theme that God's plans cannot be thwarted?

Identify God's plan, purpose, and power in His choosing to deliver Israel from evil.

PLAN:

POWER:

PURPOSE:

6. Do you agree with the statement, "The righteous shall never suffer"? Why or why not?

   Does the story of Esther reveal whether or not any Jews died in their fight for survival? (9:1-15)

7. Psalm 7:14-16 states that he who is "pregnant" with evil will bring about his own downfall. This proved to be the case in Esther. Look up the following verses and, in your own words, write down the two Scriptural principles they affirm.
   ☐ Psalm 9:15-16 *"wicked are ensnared by work of their own hands*
   ☐ Psalm 37:14-15 *wicked - their swords will pierce their own hearts*
   ☐ Psalm 54:4-7
   ☐ Psalm 57:6 *They dug a pit in my path + have fallen into it themselves*
   ☐ Proverbs 1:15-16 *sinners - do not follow their path - they rush into sin*
   ☐ Proverbs 24:12 *"will he not repay each person according to what he has done"?*

   Is it your experience that the wicked receive their just deserts?

   What is the narrator's view of the justice of God?

8. In chapter 4, does Mordecai doubt that danger is a reality and that it is imminent?

What is his conviction concerning the ultimate outcome of this tragedy?

Describe your perspective toward the evil circumstances you or your church are confronting.

9. Could the Jews have been annihilated? How does Biblical history answer this question?

10. If the principle is true that God eventually causes the destruction of the wicked, should Christians sit by and patiently wait for this to happen?

What is the message of Esther?

Was the Feast of Purim instituted to celebrate the revenge of the Jews? (9:18) Explain.

What is the godly attitude Christians should strive for toward evil and the wicked?

What is the relationship in Esther between human initiative and divine intervention?

11. What would the message of Esther have been to those Jews who first read it living scattered in a foreign land?

Do you see God's hand at work in history today? In what ways?

The conviction of Mordecai and of the Book of Esther is that God will surely deliver. Are you facing a situation where in your heart you believe it is too hopeless for God?

For Further Study
1. Make a chart of each chapter of Esther condensing the contents of each into one brief title. Memorize the chapter numbers and corresponding titles.
2. Produce a list of what God has been teaching you from your study of Esther. Ask Him to make these truths a vital part of your everyday life. Thank Him for His providence.

•TOOL CHEST•
(A Suggested Optional Resource)

WHAT THE BIBLE IS ALL ABOUT
Henrietta C. Mears' book by Regal Books should be an early addition to every Bible student's personal library. This classic introduces the reader to the main themes, lessons, and characters of each book of Scripture. It provides information about the authors as well as book outlines, maps, and other helpful aids for making sense of difficult parts of the Bible. Also included is a weekly Bible reading schedule. Mears' book is a terrific survey of the Old and New Testaments. You might read her chapter on "Understanding Esther" and compare her notes to your own study.